Hoover Institution Bibliographical Series: **XLIX**

SOUTHERN AFRICAN HISTORY BEFORE 1900:

A SELECT BIBLIOGRAPHY OF ARTICLES

by

Leonard Thompson,

Richard Elphick and Inez Jarrick

Hoover Institution Press

Stanford University . Stanford, California

The Hoover Institution on War, Revolution and Peace, founded at Stanford University in 1919 by the late President Herbert Hoover, is a center for advanced study and research on public and international affairs in the twentieth century. The views expressed in its publications are entirely those of the authors and do not necessarily reflect the views of the Hoover Institution.

Standard Book Number 8179-2491-4
Library of Congress Card Number 70-143322
Second printing, 1972
© 1971 by the Board of Trustees of the Leland Stanford Junior University
Printed in the United States of America

PREFACE

This is a select bibliography, designed by historians for historians. The journals that are listed under Journals Indexed have been covered fully, from their foundations to the most recent dates available. Articles in journals less concerned with the history of southern Africa have not been excluded, but they have not been searched systematically.

We have discarded articles which, in our judgment, are of interest almost exclusively to the archeologist or the anthropologist, or which deal with the minutiae of the history of a locality or a small community; thus the archeologist or anthropologist or local historian should not expect to find his professional needs fully satisfied here.

The articles are grouped in 26 sections, some with sub-sections. Each article is listed once only, even though many articles contain material that is relevant to more than one of the sections. We have inserted cross-references at the ends of sections, but these cross-references are not exhaustive. Users of the bibliography are therefore advised to refer to the Author Index and also to consult every section that is likely to contain items relating to their interests.

No doubt our selections and classifications reflect our own subjective views. Other contemporary historians may disagree with some of our decisions; future historians will certainly do so. But we hope that we have provided a tool that will be useful to the growing number of students and scholars who are concerned with the fascinating and complex problems of southern African history.

Several people have had a hand in this work. Gerrit Harinck began to make bibliographies for me. Richard Elphick conceived the idea of publishing this bibliography and worked out a set of criteria for the selection of articles and categories for their classification, in consultation with me and others. Inez Jarrick, helped by Jocelyn Murray, prepared a manuscript in accordance with these decisions, and Valerie Pichanick, Nina Robbins, and Sue Sturman have checked almost the entire manuscript.

We are grateful to Professor Desmond Clark and Professor Brian Fagan, who helped us to determine which archeological articles to include, and to

Dr. Martin Legassick, who placed his own bibliographical files at our disposal. Dr. Peter Duignan of the Hoover Institution gave valuable advice and coöperation. Financial support from the African Studies Center and the Senate Research Committee of the University of California, Los Angeles, and the Concilium on International and Area Studies of Yale University, made the work possible.

Yale University
December 1969

Leonard Thompson

JOURNALS INDEXED

Major Journals

The following journals have been indexed for the years stated and constitute major sources for the bibliography.

Africa, 1929-1968
African Language Studies, 1960-1967
African Notes and News, 1943-1965
Annals of the University of Stellenbosch, Series B, 1923-1963
Antiquity, 1927-1966
Archives Yearbook for South African History, 1938-1967

Bantu Studies, 1921-1941; African Studies, 1942-1967 (3)

Cape Law Journal, 1884-1900; South African Law Journal, 1900-1967 (Aug.)
Communications from the School of African Studies, University of Cape Town,
    Series 2, Nos. 1-31, 1942-1965
Communications of the University of South Africa, 1956-1968 (Series A, B, C)

Hertzog-Annale van die Suid-Afrikaanse Akademie vir Wetenskap en Kuns,
    1952-1963
Historia, 1952-1966
Historiese Studies, 1939-1949

Journal of African History, 1960-1969
Journal of African Languages, 1962-1966
Journal of the African Society, 1901-1934; Journal of the Royal African Society,
    1935-1944; African Affairs, 1945-1966 (3)
Journal of the Royal Anthropological Institute, 1872-1967
Journal of the Society for Army Historical Research, 1921-1967

NADA, The Southern Rhodesia Native Affairs Department Annual, 1923-1963;
    NADA, The Southern Rhodesia Ministry of Internal Affairs Annual, 1964-1966
Navorsinge van die Nasionale Museum, Bloemfontein, 1952-1962

Occasional Papers of the National Museum of Southern Rhodesia, relevant issues

Proceedings of the Pan-African Congress on Pre-History. Nos. 1-5

Proceedings of the Rhodesia Scientific Association, 1899-1933; Proceedings
and Transactions of the Rhodesia Scientific Association, 1933-1964

Race Relations, Nov. 1933-1950; Race Relations Journal, 1951-1962
Report of the South African Association for the Advancement of Science, 1903-
1915; South African Journal of Science, 1916-1967 (Nov.)
Rhodesiana, 1956-1968

South African Archeological Bulletin, 1945-1967 (Jan.)
South African Geographical Journal, 1917-1961
South African Journal of Economics, 1933-1966
South African Public Library. Cape Town. Quarterly Bulletin. Kwartaalblad.
1946-1966
South West Africa Scientific Society. Journal, 1925-1965

Transactions of the South African Philosophical Society, 1878-1909; Transactions of the Royal Society of South Africa, 1909-1962
Tydskrif vir Wetenskap en Kuns, 1922-1926, 1940-1960

Union of South Africa. Department of Native Affairs. Ethnological Publications;
Union (after 1961 Republic) of South Africa. Department of Bantu Administration and Development. Ethnological Publications. Nos. 1-49

Minor Journals

The following journals, while not major sources, yielded valuable material
and were systematically indexed.

English Historical Review, 1886-1967

History, 1917-1967
History Today, 1951-1967

Man, 1901-1967

School of Oriental Studies, Bulletin, 1917-1938; School of Oriental and
African Studies, Bulletin, 1939-1967
South African Quarterly, 1914-1926

Tydskrif vir Rasse-Aangeleenthede (Journal of Racial Affairs, SABRA),
1949-1965 (Jan.)

In addition to the journals which were systematically indexed, miscellaneous
articles from diverse journals are included. These articles were obtained
from the British Humanities Index, CARDAN, and private bibliographies.

CONTENTS

ABBREVIATIONS

ANN	Africana Notes and News
AS	African Studies
AYB	Archives Yearbook for South African History
BS	Bantu Studies
CUSA	Communications of the University of South Africa
EP	Union of South Africa. Department of Native Affairs. Ethnological Publications
Hertzog-Annale	Hertzog-Annale van die Suid-Afrikaanse Akademie vir Wetenskap en Kuns
HS	Historiese Studies
JAH	Journal of African History
JAS	Journal of the African Society
JRAI	Journal of the Royal Anthropological Institute
JRAS	Journal of the Royal African Society
JSAHR	Journal of the Society for Army Historical Research
JSWASS	South West Africa Scientific Society. Journal
NADA	Southern Rhodesia Native Affairs Department. Annual
Occ. Pap. Nat. Mus. S. Rhod.	Occasional Papers of the National Museums of Southern Rhodesia
Proc. Pan-Af. Cong. Pre-Hist.	Proceedings of the Pan-African Congress on Pre-History
PRSA	Proceedings of the Rhodesia Scientific Association
PTRSA	Proceedings and Transactions of the Rhodesia Scientific Association
QBSAL	South African Public Library. Cape Town. Quarterly Bulletin
RSAAAS	Report of the South African Association for the Advancement of Science
SAAB	South African Archaeological Bulletin
SABRA	Tydskrif vir Rasse-Aangeleenthede. Journal of Racial Affairs
SAGJ	South African Geographical Journal
SAJE	South African Journal of Economics

SAJS   South African Journal of Science
SALJ   South African Law Journal
SAS–UCT   Communications from the School of African Studies, University
                of Cape Town, Series 2
Stellenbosch B.   Annals of the University of Stellenbosch, Series B

TRSSA   Transactions of the Royal Society of South Africa
TWK   Tydskrif vir Wetenskap en Kuns

I HISTORIOGRAPHY AND METHODOLOGY

1. Böeseken, A. J. "In Defense of Dr. George McCall Theal: A Reply to Miss Merle Babrow," _Historia_, vol. 10, no. 1 (March 1965), 16-21.

2. _____. "Theal en sy Bronne," _Historia_, vol. 9, no. 1 (March 1964), 48-52.

3. Boxer, C. R. "S. R. Welch and his History of the Portuguese in Africa, 1495-1806," _JAH_, vol. 1, no. 1 (1960), 55-63.

4. Bryden, H. A. "South African History," _Edinburgh Review_, vol. 248, no. 505 (July 1928), 123-37.

5. Coetzee, C. G. "The Bantu and the Study of History," _Historia_, vol. 11, no. 2 (June 1966), 96-105.

6. De Ru, Annemarie. "Het Beeld van de Zuidafrikaanse Geschiedenis in Nederland van 1899-1956," _Hertzog-Annale_, vol. 7 (Dec. 1960), 74-117.

7. Du Plessis, J. S. "Gustav Schoeman Preller, 4 Okt. 1875— 6 Okt. 1943; Sy Geskiedbeskouing," _Historia_, vol. 1, no. 2 (Oct. 1956), 156-66.

8. Gann, Lewis H. "Liberal Interpretations of South African History: A Review Article," _Rhodes-Livingston Journal_, vol. 25 (March 1959), 40-58.

9. Hattersley, Alan F. "Canada and South Africa; A Plea for Inter-Dominion Historical Study," _Canadian Historical Review_, vol. 3, no. 2 (June 1922), 114-19.

10. Hunter, Monica. "Methods of Study of Culture Contact," _Africa_, vol. 7, no. 3 (July 1934), 335-50.

11. Mönnig, H. O. "The Development of Anthropology in South Africa," _Africa Institute Bulletin_, vol. 2, no. 2 (Feb. 1964), 35-41.

12. Nienaber, P. J. "Suid-Afrikaanse Plekname as studievak," _TWK_ (New Series), vol. 1, no. 2 (Dec. 1940), 131-37; vol. 4, no. 2 (Dec. 1943), 105-9.

13. _____. "Uit die Geskiedenis van ons Tydskrifte," _TWK_ (New Series), vol. 11, no. 1 (April 1951), 142-76.

14. Pelzer, A. N. "Dr. Theal oor sy eie Werk," _Historia_, vol. 10, no. 2 (June 1965), 80-82.

15. _____. "Probleme i.v.m. Navorsing oor die Geskiedenis van die Suid-Afrikaanse Republiek," _TWK_ (New Series), vol. 16, no. 1 (April 1956), 20-30.

16. Scholtz, G. D. "Die Ontwikkeling en Huidige Stand van die Afrikaanse Historiografie," _TWK_ (New Series), vol. 6, no. 3 (Nov. 1946), 30-40.

17. Spies, F. J. du T. "Die Uitwerking van Enkele Europese Geestestrominge op ons Geskiedskrywing," _Historia_, vol. 5, no. 4 (Dec. 1960), 221-30.

18. Strydom, S. "Enkele Gedagtes oor die Pleknaamstudie," _Hertzog-Annale_, vol. 6 (Dec. 1959), 59-66.

19. Thompson, L. M. "Afrikaner Nationalist Historiography and the Policy of Apartheid," _JAH_, vol. 3, no. 1 (1962), 125-41.

20. _____. "South Africa," in Winks, Robin, _The Historiography of the British Empire-Commonwealth_ (1966, Durham, North Carolina), 212-36.

21. Van Jaarsveld, F. A. "Die Afrikaner se Geskiedsbeeld," _CUSA_, B6 (1958), 33 pp.

22. _____. "Die Beeld van die Groot Trek in the Suid-Afrikaanse Geskiedskrywing, 1843-1899," _CUSA_, C42 (1963), 82 pp.

23. _____. "Die Hervertolking van ons Geskiedenis," _CUSA_, B19 (1963), 103 pp.

24. _____. "Ou en Nuwe Weë in die Suid-Afrikaanse Geskiedskrywing," _CUSA_, A16 (1961), 60 pp.

25. _____. "Tyd en Geskiedenisbeeld. 'n Metodologies-Kritiese Ondersoek na die Werk van Dr. W. J. Leyds," _TWK_ (New Series), vol. 14, no. 1 (April 1954), 97-107.

26. Van Schoor, M.C.E. "Die Biografie in die Suid-Afrikaanse Geskiedskrywing," _Historia_, vol. 4, no. 1 (Mar. 1959), 3-18.

27. Van Winter, P. J. "George McCall Theal en de Oudste Grenzen van Tulbagh," <u>ANN</u>, vol. 8, no. 4 (Sept. 1951), 122-28.

See also: X-A

II   ARCHIVES, BIBLIOGRAPHIES, AND OTHER SOURCES

28. Anon. "List of Theses in Economics and Allied Subjects Completed or in Progress in Universities and University Colleges in the Union of South Africa," <u>SAJE</u>, vol. 3, no. 3 (Sept. 1935), 465-68.

29. Botha, C. Graham. "Historical Research in South Africa with special reference to the Cape Archives," <u>RSAAAS</u>, vol. 16, no. 3 (1919), 177-85.

30. Campbell, Killie. "My Africana Collection," <u>ANN</u>, vol. 2, no. 4 (Sept. 1945), 119-21.

31. Denfield, Joseph. "Notes on Some Lost Border Newspapers," <u>QBSAL</u>, vol. 19, no. 3 (Mar. 1965), 72-79.

32. Dentz, Fred Oudschans. "Van Riebeeck-bibliographie (1753-1960)," <u>TWK</u> (New Series), vol. 20, no. 2 (Oct. 1960), 111 pp.

33. Du Preez, A. M. "List of Dissertations and Theses accepted by the University of South Africa, 1919-1958," <u>CUSA</u>, C8 (1958), 96 pp.

34. Engels, Louise J. "Personal Accounts of the Cape of Good Hope written between 1652 and 1715," <u>ANN</u>, vol. 8, no. 3 (June 1951), 71-100.

35. Hammond-Tooke, W. D. "Presidential Address: Notes on Some of the Earlier Contributions to Anthropological Work in South Africa," <u>RSAAAS</u>, vol. 5 (1908), 345-62.

36. Helly, Dorothy Oxman. "The American Board for Foreign Missions in South Africa," <u>QBSAL</u>, vol. 11, no. 4 (June 1957), 129-43.

37. Hockly, H. E. "1820 Settler Africana," <u>ANN</u>, vol. 11, no. 7 (June 1955), 243-56.

38. Holli, Melvin G. "Joseph Chamberlain and the Jameson Raid; a Bibliographical Survey," Journal of British Studies, vol. 3 (May 1964), 152-66.

39. Humphreys, J.C.N. "Gold Mining Africana," ANN, vol. 15, no. 5 (Mar. 1963), 171-81.

40. Jacques, A. A. "A Survey of Shangana-Tsonga, Ronga, and Tswa Literature," BS, vol. 14, no. 3 (Sept. 1940), 259-70.

41. Kuper, B. "Bibliography of Native Law in South Africa, 1941-1961," AS, vol. 23, no. 3-4 (1964), 155-65.

42. MacKenzie, Norman H. "South African Travel Literature in the Seventeenth Century," AYB, pt. 2 (1955), 1-112

43. Muller, C.F.J., ed. "Summaries of Theses Accepted by the University of South Africa in 1959," CUSA, C19 (1960), 50 pp.

44. Naudé, C.P.T., ed. "Summaries of Theses Accepted by the University of South Africa in 1962," CUSA, C40 (1963), 53 pp.

45. Schapera, I. "The Present State and Future Development of Ethnographical Research in South Africa," BS, vol. 8, no. 3 (Sept. 1934), 219-342.

46. Schofield, J. F. "The Manuscripts of the Rev. A. Merensky," ANN, vol. 3, no. 2 (Mar. 1946), 48-49.

47. Simpson, D. H. "A Note on the Bibliography of George McCall Theal," QBSAL, vol. 4, no. 4 (June 1950), 126-32.

48. Spohr, O. H. " 'Het Volksblad' and Dr. Wilhelm Heinrich Immanuel Bleek, 1862-1866," QBSAL, vol. 17, no. 4 (June 1963), 116-26.

49. Steyn, J. L., ed. "Summaries of Theses Accepted by the University of South Africa in 1961," CUSA, C32 (1961), 48 pp.

50. Tabler, Edward C. "Some African Diaries," ANN, vol. 2, no. 1 (Dec. 1944), 20-21; further notes in ANN, vol. 2, no. 2 (March 1945), 55-56 and ANN, vol. 6, no. 4 (Sept. 1949), 96.

51. Taylor, Alan R., and Eugene P. Dvorin. "Political Development in British Central Africa, 1890-1956; A Select Survey of the Literature and Background Materials," Race, vol. 1, no. 1 (Nov. 1959), 61-78.

52. Venter, P. J. "The Destruction of Records in South Africa," <u>AYB</u>, pt. 1 (1938), 233-39.

53. Walls, A. F. "Bibliography of the Society for African Church History, I," <u>Journal of Religion in Africa</u>, vol. 1, fasc. 1 (1967), 46-94.

See also: III, X-A

III GENERAL INTERPRETIVE ARTICLES, SURVEYS OF SOUTH AFRICAN HISTORY

54. Arkin, Marcus. "The Jewish Share in South African Economic Development," <u>SAJE</u>, vol. 24, no. 2 (June 1956), 135-43.

55. Bodenstein, H.D.J. "English Influences on the Common Law of South Africa," <u>SALJ</u>, vol. 32, pt. 4 (1915), 337-58.

56. Bradlow, Edna and Frank. "Trek and Counter-Trek in South Africa," <u>History Today</u>, vol. 9 (May 1959), 326-35.

57. Brownlee, Frank. "The Clash of Colour in South Africa," <u>JRAS</u>, vol. 37 (1938), 227-40.

58. Chorley, J. K. "A Short Historical Account of Tsetse in Southern Rhodesia," <u>PTRSA</u>, vol. 36 (Dec. 1938), 41-51.

59. Clarke, Phillis L. "Geography and Settlement in South Africa and Australia," <u>SAGJ</u>, vol. 13 (1930), 17-46.

60. Dicke, B. H. "The Tsetse-Fly's Influence on South African History," <u>SAJS</u>, vol. 29 (1932), 792-96.

61. Dittmer, Kunz. "Zur Geschichte Afrikas—3. Die ältere Geschichte Süd- und Zentralafrikas," <u>Saeculum</u>, vol. 17, no. 1-2 (1966), 37-89.

62. Du Toit, A. E. "The Earliest British Document on Education for the Coloured Races," <u>CUSA</u>, C34 (1962), 40 pp.

63. Eybers, E. "Hoofstukke uit die Geskiedenis van Opvoeding en Onderwys in Suid-Afrika," <u>TWK</u>, vol. 3 (1924-25), 232-40; vol. 4, no. 1 (Aug. 1925), 38-47; vol. 4, no. 2 (Nov. 1925), 61-71; vol. 4, no. 4 (June 1926), 211-24.

64. Gilbert, Donald Wood. "The Economic Effects of the Gold Discoveries Upon South Africa: 1886-1910," Quarterly Journal of Economics, vol. 47 (Aug. 1933), 553-97.

65. Gray, Richard. "Annular Eclipse Maps," JAH, vol. 9, no. 1 (1968), 147-57.

66. _____. "Eclipse Maps," JAH, vol. 6, no. 3 (1965), 251-62.

67. Hattersley, A. F. "Inter-Colony Migration in Early Victorian Times," SAJE, vol. 24, no. 4 (Dec. 1956), 277-89.

68. Hope, C. D. "Our Place in History," RSAAAS, vol. 4 (1907), 168-74.

69. Kahn, E. "The Right to Strike in South Africa: An Historical Analysis," SAJE, vol. 11, no. 1 (March 1943), 24-47.

70. _____. "The Study of Economic History in South Africa and the Concept of the 'Frontier Spirit'—A Review Article," SAJE, vol. 10, no. 1 (March 1942), 36-46.

71. Keppel-Jones, A. M. "Where Did We Take the Wrong Turning?" Race Relations Journal, vol. 26, no. 1 (Jan.-Mar. 1959), 18-30.

72. Kingon, John R. L. "Cattle as a Factor in the Economic Development of South Africa," RSAAAS, vol. 15 (Mar.-Apr. 1919), 425-40.

73. _____. "A Survey of Aboriginal Place-Names," RSAAAS, vol. 15 (July 1919), 712-79.

74. McCrone, I. D. "The Frontier Tradition and Race Attitudes in South Africa," Race Relations Journal, vol. 28, no. 3 (July-Sept. 1961), 19-30.

75. _____. "The Functional Analysis of a Group Attitude towards the Native," SAJS, vol. 30 (1933), 687-89.

76. _____. "Psychological Factors Affecting the Attitude of White to Black in South Africa," SAJS, vol. 27 (1930), 591-98.

77. Naudé, C.P.T. et. al. "Kulturele Kontaksituasies," CUSA, B11 (1960), 64 pp.

78. Pettman, Charles. "South African Place-Names," RSAAAS, vol. 11 (Jan. 1915), 95-106.

79. Pettman, Charles. "An Enquiry into the Derivation of Certain South African Place-Names," <u>RSAAAS</u>, vol. 12 (Dec. 1915), 159-70.

80. _____. "An Enquiry into the Origin and Derivation of Certain South African Place-Names, II," <u>RSAAAS</u>, vol. 16, no. 5 (1920), 432-42.

81. Potgieter, E. F. "Kontak in Suidelike Afrika," <u>SABRA</u>, vol. 7, no. 2 (Jan. 1956), 52-65.

82. Robb, A. M. "Geographical Influences in South African History," <u>SAGJ</u>, vol. 3, no. 1 (1919), 65-78.

83. Robertson, H. M. "The Historical Evolution of South African Wage Levels," <u>Race Relations</u>, vol. 6, no. 4 (1939), 134-37.

84. _____. "150 Years of Economic Contact Between Black and White," <u>SAJE</u>, vol. 2, no. 4 (Dec. 1934), 403-25; vol. 3, no. 1 (Mar. 1935), 3-25.

85. Rosenthal, E. "Mail Coach on the Veld: The History of Mail Coaches in South Africa," <u>ANN</u>, vol. 10, no. 3 (June 1953), 76-111.

86. Salomon, Laurence. "The Economic Background to the Revival of Afrikaner Nationalism," <u>Boston University Papers in African History</u>, vol. 1 (1964), 217-42.

87. Sayce, R. U. "The Dissemination and Agglomeration of Habitations in South Africa," <u>Geography</u>, vol. 14, no. 80 (Spring 1928), 303-7.

88. Schauder, H. "The Chemical Industry in South Africa Before Union (1910)," <u>SAJE</u>, vol. 14, no. 4 (Dec. 1946), 277-87.

89. Smit, D. E. "Emigrasie na Suid-Afrika in die 19e Eeu," <u>QBSAL</u>, vol. 16, no. 4 (June 1962), 161-64.

90. Swart, M. J. "Die Invloed van die Isolasiefaktor op die Vorming van die Afrikaner tot 1850," <u>Hertzog-Annale</u>, vol. 5 (Dec. 1958), 73-105.

91. Thompson, Leonard M. "The South African Dilemma," in Hartz, L., <u>The Founding of New Societies</u> (New York, 1964), 178-218.

92. Van Jaarsveld, F. A. "Tydgenote oor die Boer, die Onderwys en die Onderwyser (1837-1877)," <u>HS</u>, vol. 8, no. 2 (Jan. 1948), 85-97.

93. Vorster, J. D. "Burgeroffisiere in Suid-Afrika," <u>HS</u>, vol. 1, no. 2 (Oct. 1939), 31-43; vol. 1, no. 3 (Jan. 1940), 20-27.

94. Walker, Eric A. "The Cape of Good Hope and its Many Masters," <u>Mariner's Mirror</u>, vol. 25, no. 3 (July 1939), 255-78.

95. _____. "The Franchise in Southern Africa," <u>Cambridge Historical Journal</u>, vol. 11, no. 1 (1953), 93-113.

96. _____. "Relief and the European Settlement of South Africa," <u>SAJS</u>, vol. 26 (1929), 100-106.

97. Wellington, J. H. "Some Geographical Aspects of the Peopling of Africa," <u>SAJS</u>, vol. 34 (Nov. 1937), 29-60.

98. Wessels, J. W. "Development of the Administration of Justice," <u>SALJ</u>, vol. 52, pt. 1 (Feb. 1935), 11-16.

99. Wiid, J. A. "European Penetration in Southern Africa," <u>Scientia</u>, vol. 65, no. 323, ser. 4 (Mar. 1939), 162-74.

IV ARCHAEOLOGY

A. <u>General</u>

100. Brothwell, D. R. "Evidence of Early Population Change in Central and Southern Africa: Doubts and Problems," <u>Man</u>, vol. 63 (July 1963), 101-4.

101. Caton-Thompson, G. "A Commentary on Dr. Laidler's Article on Beads in Africa South of the Zambezi," <u>PTRSA</u>, vol. 34, no. 2 (Aug. 1936), 10-20.

102. Clark, J. Desmond. "Changing Trends and Developing Values in African Prehistory," <u>African Affairs</u> (Proc. ASA Conf. of the U.K. - 1964) (Spring 1965), 76-95.

103. _____. "The Prehistoric Origins of African Culture," <u>JAH</u>, vol. 5, no. 2 (1964), 161-83.

104. Clark, J. Desmond. "A Provisional Correlation of Prehistoric Cultures North and South of the Sahara," SAAB, vol. 9, no. 33 (Mar. 1954), 3-17.

105. _____. "A Note on Early River-Craft and Fishing-Practices in South-East Africa," SAAB, vol. 15, no. 59 (1960), 77-79.

106. Cooke, C. K. "Evidence of Human Migrations from the Rock Art of Southern Rhodesia," Africa, vol. 35, no. 3 (July 1965), 263-85.

107. Fagan, Brian M. "Radiocarbon Dates for Sub-Saharan Africa," JAH, vol. 2, no. 1 (1961), 137-39; vol. 4, no. 1 (1963), 127-28; vol. 6, no. 1 (1965), 107-16; vol. 7, no. 3 (1966), 495-506; vol. 8, no. 3 (1967), 513-27; vol. 10, no. 1 (1969), 149-69.

108. _____. "Early Trade and Raw Materials in South Central Africa," JAH, vol. 10, no. 1 (1969), 1-13.

109. Goodwin, A.J.H., ed. "A Commentary on the History and Present Position of South African Prehistory with Full Bibliography," BS, vol. 9, no. 4 (Dec. 1935), 291-417.

110. _____. "Earlier, Middle and Later," SAAB, vol. 1, no. 3 (July 1946), 74-76.

111. _____. "Notes on Archaeological Method with Special Reference to South African Conditions," SAS-UCT, (New Series) no. 4 (Aug. 1942), 27 pp.

112. _____. "The Stone Ages in South Africa," Africa, vol. 2, no. 2 (April 1929), 174-82.

113. Holm, Erik. "Die lewensbeskouing van die voorhistoriese mens," TWK (New Series), vol. 20, no. 1 (April 1960), 53-67.

114. Inskeep, R. R. "The Late Stone Age in Southern Africa," in Bishop, W. W., and J. D. Clark, eds., Background to Evolution in Africa (Chicago, 1967), 557-82.

115. Laidler, P. W. "Beads in Africa South of the Zambesi," PTRSA, vol. 34, no. 1 (Dec. 1934), 1-27; vol. 35, no. 1 (Aug. 1937), 35-46.

116. Malan, B. D. "Some Problems of the Stone Age in South Africa," SAJS, vol. 39 (Jan. 1943), 71-87.

117. Mason, R. J. "The Origin of South African Society," SAJS, vol. 61, no. 7 (July 1965), 255-67.

118. Schofield, J. F. "Pottery from Natal, Zululand, Bechuanaland, and South-West Africa," SAJS, vol. 35 (Dec. 1938), 382-95.

119. Sentker, H. F. "Archaeology and South Africa," Unisa (Annual Journal of the University of South Africa), vol. 21 (1967), 16-24.

120. Stuiver, Minze, and Nicolaas J. van der Merwe. "Radiocarbon Chronology of the Iron Age in Sub-Saharan Africa," Current Anthropology, vol. 9, no. 1 (Feb. 1968), 54-58.

121. Summers, Roger. "Iron Age Industries of Southern Africa, with Notes on their Chronology, Terminology, and Economic Status," in Bishop, W. W., and J. D. Clark, eds., Background to Evolution in Africa (Chicago, 1967), 687-700.

122. Thompson, Louis C. "Ingots of Native Manufacture," NADA, vol. 26 (1949), 7-19.

123. Van Riet Lowe, C. "The Smithfield 'N' Culture," TRSSA, vol. 23, no. 4 (1936), 367-72.

124. _____. "South Africa's Place in Prehistory: A Plea for Organised Research and the Better Preservation of Prehistoric Remains," SAJS, vol. 27 (Nov. 1930), 100-116.

   B. Transvaal (including Botswana and Swaziland)

125. Bates, C. W. "Archaeological Sites on the Groot Letaba River," SAJS, vol. 43 (July 1947), 365-75.

126. Caton-Thompson, G., and G. M. Morant. "Mapungubwe. 1. The Excavations and Culture. 2. The Skeletal Remains," Antiquity, vol. 13 (Sept. 1939), 324-41.

127. de Vaal, J. B. " 'n Soutpansbergse Zimbabwe, 'n Voorlopige Ondersoek van 'n Bouval op die Plaas Solvent," SAJS, vol. 40 (Nov. 1943), 303-22.

128. Fagan, Brian [M.]. "The Greefswald Sequence: Bambandyanalo and Mapungubwe," JAH, vol. 5, no. 3 (1964), 337-61.

129. Fichardt, J. "Prehistoric Cultural Material from Wellington Estate, Settlers, Springbok Flats, Transvaal," SAAB, vol. 12, no. 46 (1957), 50-61.

130. Gardner, Guy A. "Hottentot Culture on the Limpopo," SAAB, vol. 4, no. 16 (Dec. 1949), 117-21.

131. _____. "Mapungubwe, 1935-1940," SAAB, vol. 10, no. 39 (1955), 73-77.

132. _____. "Mapungubwe and the Second Volume," SAAB, vol. 13, no. 52 (1958), 123-32.

133. _____. "The Shallow Bowls of Mapungubwe," SAAB, vol. 14, no. 53 (1959), 35-37.

134. Laidler, P. W. "The Archaeology of Certain Prehistoric Settlements in the Heilbron Area," TRSSA, vol. 23, no. 1 (1935), 23-70.

135. Le Roux, S. F. "Some Iron Age Cultural Remains from the Southern Transvaal," SAAB, vol. 21, pt. 2, no. 82 (June 1966), 88-91.

136. Mason, R. J. "The Excavations of Four Caves near Johannesburg," SAAB, vol. 6, no. 23 (Sept. 1951), 71-79.

137. _____, and N. J. van der Merwe. "Radiocarbon Dating of Iron Age Sites in the Southern Transvaal: Melville Koppies and Uitkomst Cave," SAJS, vol. 60, no. 5 (May 1964), 142.

138. _____. "South African Iron Age Pottery from the Southern Transvaal," SAAB, vol. 7, no. 26 (June 1952), 70-79.

139. Partridge, T. C. "Ficus Cave: An Iron Age Living Site in the Central Transvaal," SAAB, vol. 21, pt. 3, no. 83 (Oct. 1966), 125-32.

140. Paver, F. R. "Trade and Mining in the Pre-European Transvaal," SAJS, vol. 30 (Oct. 1933), 603-11.

141. Rudner, Ione. "Archaeological Report on the Tsodilo Hills, Bechuanaland," SAAB, vol. 20, pt. 2, no. 78 (June 1965), 51-70.

142. Seddon, J. D. "Kurrichane: A Late Iron Age Site in the Western Transvaal," AS, vol. 25, no. 4 (1966), 227-31.

143. Siegrist, M. K., and D. Burn. "Potsherds from Groblerdal: A Link with Iron Age Pottery from the Southern Transvaal," <u>SAJS</u>, vol. 61, no. 8 (Aug. 1965), 297-301.

144. Van Hoepen, E. C. N., and A. C. Hoffman. "Die Oorblyfsels van Buispoort en Braklaagte, Noordwes van Zeerust," <u>Argeologiese Navorsing van die Nasionale Museum, Bloemfontein,</u> vol. 2, no. 1 (1935), 1-25.

145. Van Riet Lowe, C. "Beads of the Water," <u>BS</u>, vol. 11, no. 4 (Dec. 1937), 367-72.

146. _____. "The Glass Beads of Mapungubwe," <u>Union of South Africa Archaeological Survey Series</u>, no. 9 (1955), 22 pp.

147. _____. "Mapungubwe. First Report on Excavations in the Northern Transvaal," <u>Antiquity</u>, vol. 10 (Sept. 1936), 282-91.

See also: IV - C, D, E, F

C. <u>Orange Free State (including Lesotho)</u>

148. Pullen, R. A. "Remains from Stone-Hut Settlements in the Frankfort District, O. F. S.," <u>SAJS</u>, vol. 38 (1941), 334-44.

149. Van Riet Lowe, C., and Raymond A. Dart. "A Preliminary Report on the Stone Huts of Vechtkop," <u>JRAI</u>, vol. 57 (1927), 217-33.

150. Walton, James. "Corbelled Stone Huts in Southern Africa," <u>Man</u>, vol. 51 (Apr. 1951), 45-48.

151. _____. "Early Bafokeng Settlement in South Africa," <u>AS</u>, vol. 15, no. 1 (1956), 37-43.

152. _____. "Early Fokeng-Hlakoana Settlement at Metlaeeng, Basutoland," <u>SAAB</u>, vol. 8, no. 29 (Mar. 1953), 3-11.

153. _____. "Early Ghoya Settlement in the Orange Free State," <u>Researches of the National Museum, Bloemfontein</u>, Memoir no. 2, 40 pp.

154. _____. "Pestles, Mullers, and Querns from the Orange Free State and Basutoland," <u>SAAB</u>, vol. 8, no. 30 (June 1953), 32-39.

155. Walton, James. "Sotho Cattle Kraals," <u>SAAB</u>, vol. 13, no. 52 (1958), 133-43.

D. <u>Natal</u>

156. Schofield, J. F. "Natal Coastal Pottery from the Durban District: A Preliminary Survey," <u>SAJS</u>, vol. 32 (1935), 508-27; vol. 33 (Mar. 1937), 993-1009.

157. _____. "A Preliminary Study of the Prehistoric Beads of the Northern Transvaal and Natal," <u>TRSSA</u>, vol. 26, no. 4 (1938), 341-71.

158. _____. "A Report on the Pottery from Bambata Cave," <u>SAJS</u>, vol. 37 (Feb. 1941), 361-72.

159. Schoute-Vanneck, C. A. "The Shell Middens on the Durban Bluff," <u>SAAB</u>, vol. 13, no. 50 (1958), 43-54.

E. <u>Cape Province and South-West Africa</u>

160. Breutz, P.-L. "Stone Kraal Settlements in South Africa," <u>AS</u>, vol. 15, no. 4 (1956), 157-75.

161. Clark, J. Desmond, and James Walton. "A Late Stone Age Site in the Erongo Mountains, South West Africa," <u>Prehistoric Society, Proceedings</u> (New Series), vol. 28 (1962), 1-16.

162. Drennan, M. R., A.J.H. Goodwin, and J. F. Schofield. "Archaeology of the Oakhurst Shelter, George," <u>TRSSA</u>, vol. 25, no. 3 (1937), 229-324.

163. Fagan, Brian M. "The Glentyre Shelter and Oakhurst Re-examined," <u>SAAB</u>, vol. 15, no. 59 (1960), 80-94.

164. Grobbelaar, C. S., and A.J.H. Goodwin. "Skeletons and Implements from a Cave near Bredasdorp, Cape Province," <u>SAAB</u>, vol. 7, no. 27 (Sept. 1952), 95-107.

165. Rudner, I., and J. "A Local Late Stone Age Development," <u>SAAB</u>, vol. 9, no. 35 (Sept. 1954), 103-7.

166. Rudner, Jalmar. "The Brandberg and its Archaeological Remains," <u>JSWASS</u>, vol. 12 (1956-57), 7-44.

167. Schofield, J. F. "A Description of the Pottery from the Umgazana and Zig-zag Caves on the Pondoland Coast," TRSSA, vol. 25, no. 4 (1938), 327-32.

168. Schrire, C. "Oakhurst: A Re-examination and Vindication," SAAB, vol. 17, no. 67 (Sept. 1962), 181-95.

169. Viereck, A. "Beziehungen Zwischen Jungsteinzeitkulturen und Felsmalereien in Südwestafrika," JSWASS, vol. 15 (1960-61), 67-70.

F. Rhodesia

170. Bernhard, F. O. "Notes on the Pre-ruin Ziwa Culture of Inyanga," Rhodesiana, vol. 11 (Dec. 1964), 22-30.

171. _____. "The Ziwa Ware of Inyanga," NADA, vol. 38 (1961), 84-92.

172. Caton-Thompson, G. "Recent Excavations at Zimbabwe and Other Ruins in Rhodesia," JAS, vol. 29 (1929-30), 132-38.

173. _____. "Southern Rhodesian Ruins; Recent Archaeological Investigations," Nature, vol. 124, no. 3129 (Oct. 19, 1929), 619-21.

174. _____. "Zimbabwe," Antiquity, vol. 3 (Dec. 1929), 424-33.

175. _____. "Zimbabwe, All Things Considered," Antiquity, vol. 38 (June 1964), 99-102.

176. Cooke, C. K. "The Archaeology of the Mafungabusi Area, Gokwe, Rhodesia," PRSA, vol. 51 (1966), 51-78.

177. _____, and K. R. Robinson. "Excavations at Amadzimba Cave, Located in the Matopo Hills, Southern Rhodesia," Occ. Pap. Nat. Mus. S. Rhod., vol. 2, no. 19 (Apr. 1954), 699-728.

178. _____. "Report on Archaeological Sites, Bubye and Limpopo Valleys of Southern Rhodesia," SAAB, vol. 15, no. 59 (1960), 95-109.

179. _____. "Report on Excavations at Pomongwe and Tshangula Caves, Matopo Hills, Southern Rhodesia," SAAB, vol. 18, pt. 3, no. 71 (Nov. 1963), 73-151.

180. Cooke, C. K., R. Summers, and K. R. Robinson. "Rhodesian Prehistory Re-examined," Part II "The Iron Age," Arnoldia (Rhodesia), (Misc. Publ. Nat. Mus. S. Rhod.), vol. 2, no. 17 (Feb. 1966), 11 pp.

181. _____. "The Waterworks Site at Khami, Southern Rhodesia: Stone Age and Proto-historic," Occ. Pap. Nat. Mus. S. Rhod., Human Sciences, vol. 3, no. 21A (June 1957), 1-43.

182. Crawford, J. R. "The Monk's Kop Ossuary," JAH, vol. 8, no. 3 (1967), 373-82.

183. Dornan, S. S. "Rhodesian Ruins and Native Tradition," RSAAAS, vol. 12 (1915), 502-16.

184. Finch, E. M. "Pit People of the Inyanga Downs," PTRSA, vol. 42 (Mar. 1949), 38-58.

185. Gardner, T., L. H. Wells, and J. F. Schofield. "The Recent Archaelogy of Gokomere, Southern Rhodesia," TRSSA, vol. 28, no. 3 (1940), 219-53.

186. Garlake, P. S. "Seventeenth Century Portuguese Earthworks in Rhodesia," SAAB, vol. 21, pt. 4, no. 84 (Jan. 1967), 157-70.

187. _____. "The Value of Imported Ceramics in the Dating and Interpretation of the Rhodesian Iron Age," JAH, vol. 9, no. 1 (1968), 13-33.

188. Goodall, E. "Domestic Animals in Rock Art," PTRSA, vol. 41 (April 1946), 57-62.

189. _____. "Report on an Ancient Burial Ground, Salisbury, Southern Rhodesia," Proc. Pan-Af. Cong. Pre-Hist., vol. 4, pt. 3 (1959), 315-22.

190. Hall, R. N. "The Present Position of the Discussion as to the Origin of the Zimbabne Culture," RSAAAS, vol. 8 (1911), 325-37

191. _____, and W. G. Neal. "Architecture and Construction of Ancient Ruins in Rhodesia," PRSA, vol. 2 (1901), 5-28.

192. Jaffey, A.J.E. "A Reappraisal of the History of the Rhodesian Iron Age up to the Fifteenth Century," JAH, vol. 7, no. 2 (1966), 189-95.

193. Jones, N. "A Brief Account of the Finds Made on the Macardon Claims, West Nicolson, Gwanda District, Southern Rhodesia," PTRSA, vol. 37 (Sept. 1939), 57-61.

194. Lorch, F. B. "Zimbabwe," ANN, vol. 8, no. 4 (Sept. 1957), 107-18.

195. Mennell, F. P., and Roger Summers. "The 'Ancient Workings' of Southern Rhodesia," Occ. Pap. Nat. Mus. S. Rhod., vol. 2, no. 20 (Nov. 1955), 765-78.

196. Robins, P. A., and Anthony Whitty. "Excavations at Harleigh Farm, near Rusape, Rhodesia, 1958-1962," SAAB, vol. 21, pt. 2, no. 82 (June 1966), 61-80.

197. Robinson, K. R. "The Archaeology of the Rozwi," in Stokes, E., and R. Brown, eds., The Zambesian Past (Manchester, 1966), 3-27.

198. _____. "Bambata Ware; Its Position in the Rhodesian Iron Age in the Light of Recent Evidence," SAAB, vol. 21, pt. 2, no. 82 (June 1966), 81-85.

199. _____. "Dated Imports from the Khami Ruins, Southern Rhodesia," SAAB, vol. 16, no. 62 (June 1961), 66-67.

200. _____. "An Early Iron Age Site from the Chibi District, Southern Rhodesia," SAAB, vol. 16, no. 63 (Sept. 1961), 75-102.

201. _____. "Excavations at Khami Ruins, Matabeleland," Proc. Pan-Af. Cong. Pre-Hist., vol. 3 (1955), 357-65.

202. _____. "Four Rhodesian Iron Age Sites: A Brief Account of Stratigraphy and Finds," Occ. Pap. Nat. Mus. S. Rhod., Human Sciences, vol. 3, no. 22A (Oct. 1958), 77-119.

203. _____. "Further Excavations in the Iron Age Deposits at the Tunnel Site, Gokomere Hill, Southern Rhodesia," SAAB, vol. 18, pt. 4, no. 72 (Dec. 1963), 155-71.

204. _____. "The Leopard's Kopje Culture: A Preliminary Report on Recent Work," Arnoldia (Rhodesia) (Misc. Pub. Nat. Mus. S. Rhod.), vol. 1, no. 25 (Mar. 1965), 7 pp.

205. _____. "The Leopard's Kopje Culture; Its Position in the Iron Age of Southern Rhodesia," SAAB, vol. 21, pt. 1, no. 81 (Mar. 1966), 5-51.

206. Robinson, K. R. "Preliminary Excavations in the Vicinity of the Sinoia Caves, Lomagundi District, Rhodesia," PRSA, vol. 51 (1966), 131-55.

207. Schofield, J. F. "The Ancient Workings of South East Africa," NADA, vol. 3 (1925), 5-11.

208. _____. "Pottery from Bechuanaland and Rhodesia," TRSSA, vol. 30, no. 1 (1943), 1-16.

209. _____. "A Survey of the Recent Prehistory of Southern Rhodesia," SAJS, vol. 38 (Jan. 1941), 81-111.

210. _____. "Zimbabwe: A Critical Examination of the Building Methods Employed," SAJS, vol. 23 (Dec. 1926), 971-86.

211. Stapelton, F., and J. F. Schofield. "Pottery from the Salisbury District, Southern Rhodesia," TRSSA, vol. 26, no. 4 (1938), 321-40.

212. Summers, Roger. "Archaeology in Southern Rhodesia, 1900-1955," Proc. Pan-Af. Cong. Pre-Hist., vol. 3 (1955), 396-411.

213. _____. "The Dating of the Zimbabwe Ruins," Antiquity, vol. 29 (June 1955), 107-11.

214. _____. "Human Figures in Clay and Stone from Southern Rhodesia and Adjoining Territories," Occ. Pap. Nat. Mus. S. Rhod., Human Sciences, vol. 3, no. 21A (June 1957), 61-75.

215. _____. "Inyanga: a preliminary report," Antiquity, vol. 26 (June 1952), 71-75.

216. _____. "Iron Age Cultures in Southern Rhodesia," SAJS, vol. 47, no. 4 (Nov. 1950), 95-107.

217. _____. "The Iron Age of Southern Rhodesia," Current Anthropology, vol. 7, no. 4 (Oct. 1966), 463-69.

218. _____. "The Southern Rhodesian Iron Age (first approximations to the history of the last 2000 years)," JAH, vol. 2, no. 1 (1961), 1-13.

219. _____. "Structural Decoration in Rhodesian Ruins," Occ. Pap. Nat. Mus. S. Rhod., vol. 3, no. 22A (Oct. 1958), 148-53.

220. Summers, Roger, K. R. Robinson, and A. Whitty. "Zimbabwe Excavations, 1958," Occ. Pap. Nat. Mus. S. Rhod., Human Sciences, vol. 3, no. 23A (Dec. 1961), 157-332.

221. Von Sicard, H. "Ruins and their Traditions on the Lower Mzingwane and in the Beitbridge Area," NADA, vol. 38 (1961), 50-73.

222. Walton, James. "The Soapstone Birds of Zimbabwe," SAAB, vol. 10, no. 39 (1955), 78-84.

223. _____. "Some Features of the Monomotapa Culture," Proc. Pan-Af. Cong. Pre-Hist., vol. 3 (1955), 336-56.

224. White, F. "On the Khami Ruins, near Bulawayo," PRSA, vol. 1 (1899-1900), 11-18.

225. Whitty, Anthony. "A Classification of Prehistoric Stone Buildings in Mashonaland, Southern Rhodesia," SAAB, vol. 14, no. 54 (1959), 57-71.

226. _____. "An Iron Age Cemetery near Salisbury Kopje," Occ. Pap. Nat. Mus. S. Rhod., Human Sciences, vol. 3, no. 22A (Oct. 1958), 141-47.

227. _____. "An Iron Age Site at Coronation Park, near Salisbury," SAAB, vol. 13, no. 49 (1958), 10-20.

228. _____. "The Origins of the Stone Architecture of Zimbabwe," Proc. Pan-Af. Cong. Pre-Hist., vol. 3 (1955), 366-77.

V   LINGUISTICS

229. Anders, H. D. "Observations on Certain Sound Changes in Xhosa Derivatives from Khoisa," SAJS, vol. 33 (Mar. 1937) 921-25.

230. Bleek, D. F. "The Distribution of Bushman Languages in South Africa," in Festschrift Meinhof: Sprachwissenschaftliche und Andere Studien (Hamburg, 1927), 55-64.

231. Cole, D. T. "Doke's Classification of Bantu Languages," AS, vol. 18, no. 4 (1959), 197-213.

232. Doke, C. M. "Bantu Language Pioneers of the Nineteenth Century," AS, vol. 18, no. 1 (1959), 1-27.

233. Doke, C. M. "The Growth of Comparative Bantu Philology," AS, vol. 2, no. 1 (Mar. 1943), 41-64.

234. _____. A Preliminary Investigation into the State of the Native Languages of South Africa with Suggestions as to Research and the Development of Literature," BS, vol. 7, no. 1 (Mar. 1933), 1-98.

235. Dornan, S. S. "The Masarwas and Their Language," RSAAAS, vol. 8, no. 7 (Feb. 1912), 218-25.

236. Ehret, Christopher. "Cattle Keeping and Milking in Eastern and Southern African History: The Linguistic Evidence," JAH, vol. 8, no. 1 (1967), 1-17.

237. _____. "Sheep and Central Sudanic Peoples in Southern Africa," JAH, vol. 9, no. 2 (1968), 213-21.

238. Greenberg, Joseph H. "The Languages of Africa," International Journal of American Linguistics; Publications, vol. 29, no. 1, part II (Jan. 1963), 1-171.

239. _____. "Studies in African Linguistic Classification, III. The Position of Bantu," Southwestern Journal of Anthropology, vol. 5, no. 4 (1949), 309-17.

240. _____. "Studies in African Linguistic Classification, VI. The Click Languages," Southwestern Journal of Anthropology, vol. 6, no. 3 (1950), 223-37.

241. _____. "Studies in African Linguistic Classification, VIII. Further Remarks of Method: Revisions and Corrections," Southwestern Journal of Anthropology, vol. 10, no. 4 (1954), 405-15.

242. Guthrie, Malcolm. "Bantu Origins: A Tentative New Hypothesis," Journal of African Languages, vol. 1 pt. 1 (1962), 9-21.

243. _____. "Comparative Bantu: A Preview," Journal of African Languages, vol. 4, pt. 1 (1965), 40-45.

244. _____. "Some Developments in the Prehistory of the Bantu Languages," JAH, vol. 3, no. 2 (1962), 273-82.

245. _____. "A Two-Stage Method of Comparative Bantu Study." African Language Studies, vol. 3 (1962), 1-24.

246. Jeffreys, M.D.W. "The Batwa: Who Are They?," _Africa_, vol. 23, no. 1 (Jan. 1953), 45-54.

247. Köhler, O. "Observations on the Central Khoisan Language Group," _Journal of African Languages_, vol. 2, pt. 3 (1963), 227-34.

248. Lanham, L. W., and D. P. Hallowes. "Linguistic Relationships and Contacts Expressed in the Vocabulary of the Eastern Bushman," _AS_, vol. 15, no. 1 (1956), 45-48.

249. Lanham, L. W. "The Proliferation and Extension of Bantu Phonemic Systems Influenced by Bushman and Hottentot," _Proceedings, Ninth Annual Congress of Linguists_ (1962, Cambridge, Mass.), 382-91.

250. Lestrade, G. P. "The Classification of the Bantu Languages," _AS_, vol. 7, no. 4 (Dec. 1948), 175-84.

251. Letele, G. L. "A Preliminary Study of the Lexicological Influence of the Nguni Languages on Southern Sotho," _SAS-UCT_, (New Series), no. 12 (Mar. 1945), 67 pp.

252. Logeman, W. "Cape Dutch," _RSAAAS_, vol. 1 (1903), 439-49.

253. Louw, J. A. "The Development of the Bantu Languages in South Africa," _Africa Institute Bulletin_, vol. 3, no. 5 (June 1963), 133-41.

254. _____. "The Nomenclature of Cattle in South Eastern Bantu Languages," _CUSA_, C2 (1957), 19 pp.

255. Macnab, Roy. "The Emergence of Afrikaans as a Literary Language," _Journal of the Royal Society of Arts_, vol. 105, no. 5000 (Mar. 29, 1957), 372-84.

256. Maingard, L. F. "A Comparative Study of Naron, Hietshware, and Korana," _AS_, vol. 22, no. 3 (1963), 97-108.

257. _____. "The Linguistic Approach to South African Prehistory and Ethnology," _SAJS_, vol. 31 (Nov. 1934), 117-43.

258. _____. "Some Linguistic Problems of South Africa," _SAJS_, vol. 26 (Dec. 1929), 835-65.

259. Nienaber, G. S. " 'n Ou ongepubliseerde lys Hottentot- en Xhosawoorde," _AS_, vol. 19, no. 3 (1960), 157-68.

260. Norton, W. A. "The Study of South African Native Languages," RSAAAS, vol. 11 (July 1915), 384-95.

261. Tucker, A. N. "Sotho-Nguni Orthography and Tone-Marking," Bulletin of the School of Oriental and African Studies (London), vol. 13, pt. 1 (1949-50), 200-224.

262. Van der Merwe, D. F., and I. Schapera. "A Comparative Study of Kgalagadi, Kwena and Other Sotho Dialects," SAS-UCT, (New Series), no. 9 (Aug. 1943), 119 pp.

263. Van Warmelo, N. J. "Early Bantu Ethnography from a Philological Point of View," Africa, vol. 3, no. 1 (Jan. 1930), 31-47.

264. _____. "Kinship Terminology of the South African Bantu," EP, no. 2, 119 pp.

265. _____. "Language Map of South Africa," EP, no. 27, 20 pp.

266. Werner, A. "Note on Clicks in the Bantu Languages," JAS, vol. 2 (1902-03), 416-21. Editorial note, pp. 422-24, and vol. 4 (1904-05), 142-43.

267. Westphal, E.O.J. "The Linguistic Prehistory of Southern Africa: Bush, Kwadi, Hottentot, and Bantu Linguistic Relationships," Africa, vol. 33, no. 3 (July 1963), 237-65.

268. _____. "On Classifying Bushman and Hottentot Languages," African Language Studies, vol. 3 (1962), 30-48.

269. _____. "A Re-Classification of Southern African Non-Bantu Languages," Journal of African Languages, vol. 1, pt. 1 (1962), 1-8.

VI   TRAVELERS AND EXPLORERS IN SOUTHERN AFRICA

270. Agar-Hamilton, J.A.I. "An African Centenary," Race Relations, vol. 8, no. 1 (1941), 6-12.

271. Anon. " 'Travels in Southern Africa in the Years 1803-1806' by Henry Lichtenstein," Quarterly Review, vol. 8 (Dec. 1812), 374-95.

272. Barber, Mary Elizabeth. "Wanderings in South Africa by Sea and Land, 1879," QBSAL, vol. 17, no. 2 (Dec. 1962), 39-53; vol. 17, no. 3 (Mar. 1963), 61-74; vol. 17, no. 4 (June 1963), 103-16; vol. 18, no. 1 (Sept. 1963), 3-17; vol. 18, no. 2 (Dec. 1963), 55-68.

273. Barnard, C. J. "Robert Jacob Gordon se Loopbaan aan die Kaap," AYB, pt. 1 (1950), 319-446.

274. Booth, Alan R. "American Whalers in South African Waters," SAJE, vol. 32, no. 4 (Dec. 1964), 278-82.

275. Duckworth, Dennis. "The Log-Book of William Paterson," ANN, vol. 12, no. 6 (June 1957), 191-97.

276. Elton, Frederick. "Journal of an Exploration of the Limpopo River," Journal of the Royal Geographical Society, vol. 42 (1872), 1-49.

277. Forbes, Vernon S. "Africana in the Sloane Collection, British Museum," QBSAL, vol. 6, no. 1 (Sept. 1951), 9-17.

278. _____. "Beutler's Expedition into the Eastern Cape, 1752," AYB, pt. 1 (1953), 269-320.

279. _____. "Colonel R. J. Gordon's Contribution to Cape Geography, 1777-1795," SAGJ, vol. 31 (1949), 3-35.

280. _____. "Dr. H. Lichtenstein's Vaccination Tour, 1805," ANN, vol. 13, no. 7 (Sept. 1959), 272-82.

281. _____. "The French Landing at Algoa Bay, 1752," ANN, vol. 16, no. 1 (Mar. 1964), 3-19.

282. _____. "John Elliott's Visit to Cape Town, 1778-1779," QBSAL, vol. 7, no. 1 (Sept. 1952), 13-19.

283. _____. "Le Vaillant's Travels," SAGJ, vol. 32 (1950), 32-51.

284. _____. "Masson's Travels," SAGJ, vol. 29 (1947), 16-31.

285. _____. "Paterson's Travels," SAGJ, vol. 30 (1948), 52-70.

286. _____. "Some Early Maps of South Africa 1595-1795," Tydskrif vir Aardrykskunde, vol. 2, no. 6 (April 1965), 9-20.

22

287. Forbes, Vernon S. "Some Visits of English Ships to the Cape, 1679-1703," QBSAL, vol. 7, no. 2 (Dec. 1952), 41-48.

288. _____. "Sparrman's Travels," SAGJ, vol. 27 (1945), 39-64.

289. _____. "Thunberg's Travels," SAGJ, vol. 28 (1946), 39-63.

290. Fripp, C. E. "Bishop Knight Bruce's Journey to the Zambesi in 1888," NADA, vol. 16 (1939), 76-91.

291. Grönberg, Gösta. "Johan August Wahlberg and His Travels in South Africa. On The Hundredth Anniversary of His Birth," ANN, vol. 8, no. 2 (Mar. 1951), 40-51.

292. Holt, Basil. "The Journal and Letters of Captain Sidney Turner," QBSAL, vol. 9, no. 1 (Sept. 1954), 1-7.

293. Jorissen, E.J.P. "Brokstukke uit die Reisbeskrywing van Dr. E.J.P. Jorissen," TWK, (New Series) vol. 6, no. 2 (May 1946), 32-51.

294. Lacy, George. "A Century of Exploration in South Africa," JAS, vol. 1 (1901-02), 215-29.

295. Lord, W. B. and T. Baines. "Shifts and Expedients of Camp Life," Rhodesiana, vol. 9 (Dec. 1963), 44-51.

296. Masson, Francis. "Mr. Masson's Botanical Travels," Philosophical Transactions, of the Royal Society of London, vol. 66, pt. 1 (1776), 268-317.

297. Ploeger, J. "Herinneringe van Hendrik Stiemens aan Natal en die Oranje-Vrystaat, met Gedeeltelike Vermelding van sy Wederwaardighede in Transvaal (1856-1879)," Hertzog-Annale, vol. 3 (Dec. 1956), 118-56.

298. Raven-Hart, R. "East Indian Voyage by Wouter Schouten," ANN, vol. 16, no. 7 (Sept. 1965), 263-78.

299. _____. "Journal and Diary by Christophorus Schweitzer," QBSAL, vol. 20, no. 3 (Mar. 1966), 84-89.

300. _____. "The New East-Indian Voyage of Christoffel Langhansz," QBSAL, vol. 19, no. 4 (June 1965), 119-39.

301. Raven-Hart, R. "Travels by Volquardt Iversen," _ANN_, vol. 16, no. 5 (Mar. 1965), 183-89.

302. Robinson, A. M. L., ed. "A Voyage to the Cape of Good Hope in 1687," _QBSAL_, vol. 4, no. 4 (June 1950), 113-22.

303. Rochlin, S. A. "Andrew Wyley: A Geologist's View of Cape Life in 1857-8," _ANN_, vol. 14, no. 4 (Dec. 1960), 133-40.

304. _____. "Oriental Impressions of the pre-1900 Cape of Good Hope," _ANN_, vol. 13, no. 4 (Dec. 1958), 132-40.

305. Ruzicka, K. F. "Dr. Emil Holub, the great Czech traveller in South Africa," _ANN_, vol. 10, no. 2 (Mar. 1953), 39-50.

306. Spies, F. J. du T. "Reisbriewe van Dr. Hendrik P. N. Muller: 1898," _Hertzog-Annale_, vol. 2 (Dec. 1955), 101-52.

307. Tabler, E. C. "Historic Route from the Lower Botletle River to the Chobe River," _ANN_, vol. 12, no. 2 (June 1956), 35-43.

308. _____. "The Hunters' Road: Shoshong to the Matabele Capital," _ANN_, vol. 11, no. 3 (June 1954), 69-80.

309. _____. "The Hunters' Road: Khami River to the Hunyani River," _ANN_, vol. 11, no. 4 (Sept. 1954), 121-32.

310. _____. "Non-Europeans as Interior Men," _ANN_, vol. 13, no. 8 (Dec. 1959), 291-96.

311. _____. "Sir Richard Glyn's Journey to the Zambezi, 1863," _ANN_, vol. 6, no. 4 (Sept. 1949), 92.

312. _____. "The South African Diary of Thomas Leask," _ANN_, vol. 6, no. 2 (Mar. 1949), 37-40.

313. _____. "The Walvis Bay Road: Rietfontein to Lake Ngami," _ANN_, vol. 12, no. 4 (Dec. 1956), 123-29.

314. _____. "The Westbeech Road: Tati to Nwasha Pan," _ANN_, vol. 11, no. 6 (Mar. 1955), 183-87.

315. _____. "The Western Old Lake Route: Shoshong to the Zambezi," _ANN_, vol. 11, no. 8 (Sept. 1955), 297-309.

316. Wallenberg, Jacob. "The Travels of a Busybody at the Cape,"
      QBSAL, vol. 2, no. 2 (Dec. 1947), 36-49; vol. 2, no. 3
      (Mar. 1948), 69-75.

      See also: VIII, X-G, X-H, XI, XII, XIII, XIV, XXIII

VII   THE SAN

317. Brownlee, F. "The Social Organization of the Kung (!un) Bush-
      men of the North-Western Kalahari," Africa, vol. 14, no. 3
      (July 1943), 124-29.

318. Cooke, C. K. "A Comparison between the Weapons in Rock Art
      in Southern Rhodesia and Weapons Known to Have been Used by
      Bushmen and Later People," Occ. Pap. Nat. Mus. S. Rhod.,
      Human Sciences, vol. 3, no. 22A (Oct. 1958), 120-40.

319. Crosby, Oscar T. "Bushmen and Ovambo in South West Africa,"
      JAS, vol. 30 (Oct. 1931), 344-60.

320. Dart, Raymond A. "The Hut Distribution Genealogy and Homo-
      geneity of the /?auni-Zkhomani Bushmen," BS, vol. 11, no. 3
      (Sept. 1937), 159-74.

321. Dornan, S. S. "The Tati Bushmen (Masarwas) and Their
      Language," JRAI, vol. 47 (Jan.-June 1917), 37-112.

322. Fourie, L. "Preliminary Notes on Certain Customs of the Hei-
      //om Bushmen," JSWASS, vol. 1 (1925-26), 49-63.

323. Hall, R. N. "Antiquity of the Bushman Occupation of Rhodesia,"
      PRSA, vol. 11, no. 3 (1912), 140-50.

324. Hirschberg, Walter. "The Problem of Relationship between
      Pygmies and Bushmen," Africa, vol. 7, no. 4 (Oct. 1934),
      444-51.

325. Hoogenhout, P. G. "The Strandlopers of South-West Africa,"
      Race Relations, vol. 16, no. 2 (1949), 38-41.

326. Lebzelter, Viktor. "Die Bushmänner Südwestafrikas," Africa,
      vol. 7, no. 1 (Jan. 1934), 70-81.

327. Maingard, L. F. "The First Contacts of the Dutch with the Bushmen until the Time of Simon van der Stel (1686)," SAJS, vol. 32 (Nov. 1935), 479-87.

328. Marshall, Lorna. "!Kung Bushman Bands," Africa, vol. 30, no. 4 (Oct. 1960), 325-55.

329. _____. "!Kung Bushman Religious Beliefs," Africa, vol. 32, no. 3 (July 1962), 221-52.

330. _____. "Marriage Among !Kung Bushmen," Africa, vol. 29, no. 4 (Oct. 1959), 335-65.

331. _____. "N!ow," Africa, vol. 27, no. 3 (July 1957), 232-40.

332. _____. "Sharing, Talking, and Giving: Relief of Social Tensions among !Kung Bushmen," Africa, vol. 31, no. 3 (July 1961), 231-49.

333. Schapera, I. "A Survey of the Bushman Question," Race Relations, vol. 6, no. 2 (1939), 68-83.

334. Schmidt, P. W. "Zur Erforschung der Alten Buschmann-Religion," Africa, vol. 2, no. 3 (July 1929), 291-301.

335. Tobias, P. V. "Bushman Hunter-Gatherers: A Study in Human Ecology," in Davis, D.H.S., ed., Ecological Studies in Southern Africa (The Hague, 1964), 67-86.

336. _____. "Bushmen of the Kalahari," Man, vol. 57 (Mar. 1957), 33-40.

337. _____. "On the Survival of the Bushmen," Africa, vol. 26, no. 2 (April 1956), 174-86.

338. Vedder, H. "Zur Vorgeschichte der Eingeborenen Völkerschaften von Südwestafrika. I. Buschmänner," JSWASS, vol. 1, no. 1 (1925-26), 5-16.

See also: IV-A, V, VIII, X-F, X-I

339. Du Plessis, J. "The Name 'Hottentot' in the Records of Early Travelers," SAJS, vol. 29 (Oct. 1932), 660-67.

340. _____. "Origin and Meaning of the Name 'Hottentot'," RSAAAS, vol. 14 (Nov. 1917), 189-93.

341. Goodwin, A.J.H. "Commentary on 'Jan van Riebeeck and the Hottentots'," SAAB, vol. 7, no. 26 (June 1952), 86-91.

342. _____. "Jan van Riebeeck and the Hottentots, 1652-62," SAAB, vol. 7, no. 25 (March 1952), 2-53.

343. _____. "Metal Working among the Early Hottentots," SAAB, vol. 11, no. 42 (1956), 16-51.

344. Hewitt, J. "Notes Relating to Aboriginal Tribes of the Eastern Province," RSAAAS, vol. 17, no. 3-4 (1921), 304-21.

345. Hodgson, M. L. "The Hottentots in South Africa to 1828: A Problem in Labour and Administration," RSAAAS, vol. 21 (Nov. 1924), 594-621.

346. Hoernlé, A. Winifred. "The Social Organization of the Nama Hottentots of South West Africa," American Anthropologist (New Series), vol. 27, no. 1 (Jan.-Mar. 1925), 1-24.

347. Kirby, Percival R. "The Swimming-Log of the Hottentots," ANN, vol. 9, no. 4 (Sept. 1952), 107-23.

348. Maingard, L. F. "The Origin of the Word 'Hottentot'," BS, vol. 9, no. 1 (March 1935), 63-67.

349. Meiring, A.J.D. "Die Hottentotte aan die Kaap voor die tyd Van Riebeeck soos opgeteken deur Jodocus Hondius," Navorsinge van die Nasionale Museum, Bloemfontein, vol. 1, no. 3 (Oct. 1953), 35-40.

350. Nienaber, G. S. " 'n Lysie Hottentotse Woorde uit 1626," AS, vol. 21, no. 1 (1962), 28-39.

351. _____. "The Origin of the Name 'Hottentot'," AS, vol. 22, no. 2 (1963), 65-90.

352. Nienaber, G. S. "Die Vroegste Verslae Aangaande Hottentots," AS, vol. 15, no. 1 (1956), 29-35.

353. Pettman, Charles. "Hottentot Place-Names," RSAAAS, vol. 17, no. 3-4 (1921), 334-52.

354. _____. "Hottentot Place-Names, II," RSAAAS, vol. 19 (1922), 372-82.

355. Raven-Hart, R. "Johan Schreyer's Description of the Hottentots, 1679," QBSAL, vol. 19, no. 2 (Dec. 1964), 56-69; vol. 19, no. 3 (Mar. 1965), 88-101.

356. R.[obinson], A. M. L. "Diary of the Missionaries at Baviaans Kloof, Cape of Good Hope, of the Year 1795," QBSAL, vol. 8, no. 2 (Dec. 1953), 51-57; vol. 8, no. 3-4 (Mar.-June 1954), 79-87.

357. Schapera, I. "A Preliminary Consideration of the Relationship between the Hottentots and the Bushmen," SAJS, vol. 23 (Dec. 1926), 833-66.

358. Tobias, P. V. "The Physical Anthropology and Somatic Origins of the Hottentots," AS, vol. 14, no. 1 (1955), 1-15.

359. Van Vreeden, B. F. "Die Khoisan Naamgewing in Griekwaland—Wes," Tydskrif vir Volkskunde en Volkstaal, vol. 21, no. 4 (Oct. 1965), 12-32.

360. Vedder, H. "Die Bergdama in Südwest-Afrika," Africa, vol. 3, no. 2 (April 1930), 178-90.

361. _____. "Zur Vorgeschichte der Eingeborenen Völkerschaften von Südwestafrika. II. Die Hottentotten," JSWASS, vol. 1 (1925-26), 37-48.

362. _____. "Zur Vorgeschichte der Völker Südwestafrikas. III. Die Bergdama," JSWASS, vol. 2 (1926-27), 35-48.

363. Willcox, A. R. "Sheep and Sheep-Herders in South Africa," Africa, vol. 36, no. 4 (Oct. 1966), 432-38.

See also: V, X-I

364. Barnard, S. P. "Voorstel vir 'n Verbond tussen Waterboer en Adam Kok, en die Daarop volgende Verdrag," TWK, vol. 1 (1922-23), 104-8.

365. De Kock, W. J. "Vyf Ongepubliseerde Briewe van Hendrik Witbooi," HS, vol. 6, no. 4 (Dec. 1945), 195-212.

366. Frey, C. "Jonker Afrikaner and His Time," JSWASS, vol. 1 (1925-26), 17-36.

367. Jod, Petrus. "Das Witbooi-Volk und die Gründung Gibeons," JSWASS, vol. 16 (1961-62), 81-98.

368. Kreft, H.H.G. "The Diary of Hendrik Witbooi," JSWASS, vol. 2 (1926-27), 49-62.

369. Lehmann, Rudolf von F. "Jonker Afrikaner und die Herero-Missionare seiner Zeit als 'Hauptlinge wider willen' (1844-1861), Südwestafrika," Veröff Museum für Völkerkunde, Leipzig, vol. 11 (1961), 410-31.

370. Maingard, L. F. "The Korana Dialects," AS, vol. 23, no. 2 (1964), 57-66.

371. _____. "Studies in Korana History, Customs, and Language," BS, vol. 6, no. 2 (June 1932), 103-62.

372. Oberholster, J. J. "Die Anneksasie van Griekwaland-Wes," AYB (1945), 1-337.

373. _____, and Basil Humphreys. "Die Campbell-Sendingkerkie," Historia, vol. 6, no. 4 (Dec. 1961), 235-48.

374. Rochlin, S. A. "Aspects of Islam in Nineteenth-Century South Africa," Bulletin of the School of Oriental and African Studies (London), vol. 10, pt. 1 (1939), 213-21.

375. _____. "Early Arabic Printing at the Cape of Good Hope," Bulletin of the School of Oriental and African Studies (London), vol. 7, pt. 1 (1933), 49-54.

376. _____. "The First Mosque at the Cape," SAJS, vol. 33 (Mar. 1937), 1100-103.

377. Schutte, C.E.G. "Dr. John Philip's Observations Regarding the Hottentots of South Africa," <u>AYB</u>, pt. 1 (1940), 89-256.

378. Secretariat of the United Nations. "The Rehoboth Community of South West Africa," <u>AS</u>, vol. 14, no. 4 (1955), 175-200.

379. Tylden, G. "The Cape Coloured Regular Regiments, 1793 to 1870," <u>ANN</u>, vol. 7, no. 2 (March 1950), 37-59.

380. _____. "The Cape Mounted Riflemen, 1827-1870," <u>JSAHR</u>, vol. 17 (1938), 227-31.

<u>See also</u>: V, X-F, X-I, XIII, XIV, XVIII, XXII

X THE BANTU-SPEAKING PEOPLES OF SOUTHERN AFRICA

A. <u>General</u>

381. Bryant, A. T. "Some South-Bantu Nation-Builders," <u>South African Quarterly</u>, vol. 7, no. 3-4 (July 25-Feb. 26, 1925-26), 18-22.

382. Child, H. F. "The History and Extent of Recognition of Native Law in Southern Rhodesia," <u>NADA</u>, vol. 40 (1963), 29-45.

383. Dornan, S. S. "Some African Burial Customs," <u>PRSA</u>, vol. 9 (1910), 88-127.

384. Dulcken, Albert C. "Appeals in Native Cases," <u>Cape Law Journal</u>, vol. 8 (1891), 204-10.

385. Du Toit, A. E. "The Earliest South African Documents on the Education and Civilization of the Bantu," <u>CUSA</u>, C47 (1963), 91 pp.

386. Eisenstadt, S. N. "African Age Groups: A Comparative Study," <u>Africa</u>, vol. 24, no. 2 (April 1954), 100-113.

387. Elsdon-Dew, R. "Serological Differences Between Various Groups of the Bantu of Southern Africa," <u>BS</u>, vol. 8, no. 4 (Dec. 1934), 361-66.

388. Garbutt, H. W. "Notes on the Natives of Rhodesia," <u>RSAAAS</u>, vol. 11 (1914), 329-36.

389. Gluckman, M. "Mortuary Customs and the Belief in a Survival after Death among the South-Eastern Bantu," BS, vol. 11, no. 2 (June 1937), 117-36.

390. _____. "Social Aspects of First Fruits Ceremonies among the South-Eastern Bantu," Africa, vol. 11, no. 1 (Jan. 1938) 25-41.

391. Hiernaux, Jean. "Bantu Expansion: The Evidence from Physical Anthropology Confronted with Linguistic and Archaeological Evidence," JAH, vol. 9, no. 4 (1968), 505-15.

392. Hutchinson, Bertram. "Some Social Consequences of Nineteenth Century Missionary Activity among the South African Bantu," Africa, vol. 27, no. 2 (April 1957), 160-77.

393. Junod, Henri [P.]. "The Condition of the Natives of South-East Africa in the Sixteenth Century, According to the Early Portuguese Documents," RSAAAS, vol. 10 (1913), 137-61.

394. Kingon, J.R.L. "Unrealised Factors in Native Economic Development," RSAAAS, vol. 15, no. 7 (May-June 1919), 506-24.

395. Kruger, F. "Das Recht der Sotho-Chuana Gruppe der Bantu in Süd Afrika," Mitteilungen des Seminars für Orientalische Sprachen (Berlin), vol. 38, no. 3 (1935), 53-114.

396. Lewin, Julius. "A Short Survey of Native Law in South Africa," BS, vol. 15, no. 2 (1941), 65-90.

397. Miracle, Marvin P. "The Introduction and Spread of Maize in Africa," JAH, vol. 6, no. 1 (1965), 39-55.

398. Norton, G. R. "The Emergence of New Religious Organisations in South Africa: A Discussion of Causes," JRAS, vol. 39 (1940), 348-53; vol. 40 (1941), 48-67.

399. Norton, W. A. "Bantu Place Names in Africa," RSAAAS, vol. 13, no. 6 (1917), 264-77.

400. Oliver, Roland. "The Problem of the Bantu Expansion," JAH, vol. 7, no. 3 (1966), 361-76.

401. Schapera, Isaac. "The Activities of Tribal Governments," in McEwan, P.J.M., and R. B. Sutcliffe, eds., The Study of Africa (London, 1965), 98-106.

402. Simons, H. J. "Marriage and Succession among Africans," Acta Juridica (1960), 312-33.

403. _____. "The Status of Customary Unions," Acta Juridica (1961), 17-37.

404. Tylden, G. "Three Mountains: Thaba Bosiu, Morosi's Mountain, Sekukuni's Mountain," ANN, vol. 9, no. 2 (Mar. 1952), 36-47.

405. Van Warmelo, N. J. "A Preliminary Survey of the Bantu Tribes of South Africa," EP 5, 123 + ix pp. + 24 maps.

406. Von Sicard, H. "Tentative Chronological Tables," NADA, vol. 23 (1946), 30-35.

407. Wright, E. Blackwood. "Native Races in South Africa," JAS, vol. 2 (1902-03), 261-75.

See also: V

B. Southern Nguni

408. Brownlee, W. T. "The Transkeian Territories of South Africa: Notes on Native Law and Customs," JAS, vol. 24 (1924-25), 110-16; 213-18.

409. De Jager, E. J. "Die Geskiedenis van die Ama-Xhosa en Ama-Thembu," Historia, vol. 9, no. 3 (Sept. 1964), 215-27.

410. Dugmore, H. H. "Kafir Government, and its Practical Operation," Cape Law Journal, vol. 7 (1890), 23-35.

411. Hammond-Tooke, W. D. "Segmentation and Fission in Cape Nguni Political Units," Africa, vol. 35, no. 2 (April 1965), 143-67.

412. _____. "The Morphology of Mpondomise Descent Groups," Africa, vol. 38, no. 1 (Jan. 1968), 26-46.

413. _____. "The Tribes of King William's Town District," EP 41, 148 pp.

414. _____. "The Tribes of Mount Frere District," EP 33, 80 pp.

415.   Hammond-Tooke, W. D. "The Tribes of Umtata District,"
       EP 35, 76 pp.

416.   _____. "The Tribes of Willowvale District," EP 36, 91 pp.

417.   _____. "The Transkeian Council System 1895-1955: an
       appraisal," JAH, vol. 9, no. 3 (1968), 455-77.

418.   Hunter, Monica. "The Effects of Contact with Europeans on
       the Status of Pondo Women," Africa, vol. 6, no. 3 (July 1933),
       259-76.

419.   Kingon, J. R. L. "Some Place-Names of Tsolo," RSAAAS,
       vol. 13, no. 2 (July 1917), 603-19.

420.   Kirby, P. R. "Gqoma, Mdepa, and the AmaTshomane Clan:
       A By-Way of Miscegenation in South Africa," AS, vol. 13,
       no. 1 (1954), 1-24.

421.   Lestrade, G. P. "Some Notes on the Political Organisation of
       Certain Xhosa-Speaking Tribes in the Transkeian Territories,"
       TRSSA, vol. 24, no. 4 (1937), 281-301.

422.   Raum, O. F. "Von Stammespropheten zu Sektenführern," in
       Benz, E., ed., Messianische Kirchen, Sekten und Bewegungen
       im Heutigen Afrika (Leiden, 1965), 47-70.

423.   Soga, J. H. "Ama-Mbo Genealogical Tables," BS, vol. 3, no. 1
       (July 1927), 49-56.

424.   Wilson, Monica. "The Early History of the Transkei and
       Ciskei," AS, vol. 18, no. 4 (1959), 167-79.

       See also: V, VIII, XIV, XVIII

C. Northern Nguni (including the Ngoni)

425.   Beemer, Hilda. "The Development of the Military Organiza-
       tion in Swaziland," Africa, vol. 10, no. 1 (Jan. 1937), 55-74;
       vol. 10, no. 2 (April 1937), 176-205.

426.   Beidelman, T. O. "Swazi Royal Ritual," Africa, vol. 36, no. 4
       (Oct. 1966), 373-405.

427. Bryant, A. T. "The Zulu Family and State Organization," <u>BS</u>, vol. 2, no. 1 (Aug. 1923), 47-51.

428. Callaway, Rev. Canon H. "Nursery Tales, Traditions and History of the Zulus in Their Own Words, with a Translation into English and Notes," <u>Memoirs of the Folklore Society</u> (Natal and London), No. 1 (1868).

429. Chadwick, J.C.C. "A Native Lawsuit in Natal," <u>Cape Law Journal</u>, vol. 9 (1892), 30-36.

430. Cook, P.A.W. "History and Izibongo of the Swazi Chiefs," <u>BS</u>, vol. 5, no. 2 (June 1931), 181-201.

431. Gluckman, Max. "The Kingdom of the Zulu of South Africa," in Fortes, M., and E. E. Evans-Pritchard, eds., <u>African Political Systems</u> (London, 1940), 25-55.

432. _____. "The Rise of a Zulu Empire," <u>Scientific American</u>, vol. 202, no. 4 (April 1960), 157-68.

433. Hammond-Tooke, W. D. "Notes on the East Coast Bantu of Eighty Years Ago," <u>RSAAAS</u>, vol. 8 (1911), 80-91.

434. Holleman, J. F. "Die Twee-eenheidsbeginsel in die Sosiale en Politieke Samelewing van die Zulu," <u>BS</u>, vol. 14, no. 1 (Mar. 1940), 31-75.

435. _____. "Die Zulu Isigodi," <u>BS</u>, vol. 15, no. 2 (June 1941), 91-118.

436. _____. "Die Zulu Isigodi (Deel II)," <u>BS</u>, vol. 15, no. 3 (Sept. 1941), 245-76.

437. Jeffreys, M.D.W. "An Early Reference to the Zulu," <u>AS</u>, vol. 25, no. 3 (1966), 159-60.

438. Junod, H. P. "Some Notes on Tshopi Origins," <u>BS</u>, vol. 3, no. 1 (July 1927), 57-71.

439. Kotze, D. J. "Die Eerste Amerikaanse Sendelinge onder die Matabeles," <u>AYB</u>, pt. 1 (1950), 129-318.

440. _____. "Die Eerste Amerikaanse Sendelinge onder die Zoeloes (1835-1838)," <u>AYB</u>, pt. 1 (1958), vii-214.

441. Kuper, Hilda. "The Development of a Primitive Nation," BS, vol. 15, no. 4 (Dec. 1941), 339-68.

442. _____. "A Ritual of Kingship among the Swazi," Africa, vol. 14, no. 5 (Jan. 1944), 230-57.

443. Lancaster, D. Gordon. "Tentative Chronology of the Ngoni, Genealogy of Their Chiefs, and Notes," JRAI, vol. 67 (1937), 77-90.

444. Mason, A. Weir. "A Native Lawsuit in Natal," Cape Law Journal, vol. 8 (1891), 144-55.

445. Meyler, H. M. "The Zulu: The Gentleman of the African Veld," JAS, vol. 24 (1924-25), 202-12.

446. Mhlanga, Wilson. "(1) The Story of Ngwaqazi. (2) The History of the Amatshangana," NADA, vol. 25 (1948), 70-73.

447. Moloja. "The Story of the 'Fetcani horde', by One of Them-selves—Moloja, of Jozani's village, at Masite, near Morija, Basutoland," Cape Quarterly Review, vol. 1, no. 2 (Jan. 1882), 267-75.

448. Myburgh, A. C. "Die Stamme van die Distrik Carolina," EP 34, 329 pp.

449. _____. "The Tribes of Barberton District," EP 25, 146 pp.

450. Nhlapo, J. M. "The Story of Amanhlapo," AS, vol. 4, no. 2 (June 1945), 97-101.

451. Nyembezi, C.L.S. "The Historical Background of the Izibongo of the Zulu Military Age," AS, vol. 7, no. 2-3 (June-Sept. 1948), 111-25; vol. 7, no. 4 (Dec. 1948), 157-74.

452. Oberholzer, M. O. "Die Opkoms van die Zoeloes," Historia, vol. 5, no. 1 (Mar. 1960), 57-66.

453. Okoye, Felix N. C. "Dingane: A Reappraisal," JAH, vol. 10, no. 2 (1969), 221-35.

454. Poole, E.H.L. "The Date of the Crossing of the Zambezi by the Ngoni," JAS, vol. 29 (1929-30), 290-92.

455. Read, Margaret. "Songs of the Ngoni People," <u>BS</u>, vol. 11, no. 1 (1937), 1-35.

456. _____. "Tradition and Prestige among the Ngoni," <u>Africa</u>, vol. 9, no. 4 (Oct. 1936), 453-84.

457. Smit, J. J. "Silkaats, die Stigter van die Matabelestam," <u>Historia</u>, vol. 5, no. 4 (Dec. 1960), 266-70.

458. Stander, H. "Die Verhouding tussen die Boere en Zoeloe tot die dood van Mpande in 1872," <u>AYB</u>, pt. 2 (1964), 199-395.

459. Stuart, P. A. "Zulu Anecdotes and Sayings," <u>NADA</u>, vol. 20 (1943), 18-23.

460. Van Warmelo, N. J., ed. "History of Matiwane and the Amangwane Tribe as told by Msebenzi to his kinsman Albert Hlongwane," <u>EP</u> 7, 275 pp.

461. _____. "Shaka's Grave at Stanger," <u>AS</u>, vol. 2, no. 2 (June 1943), 108-12.

462. Van Zyl, M. C. "Dinizulu se Vlug na die Suid-Afrikaanse Republiek in 1888," <u>CUSA</u>, C 30 (1961), 39 pp.

463. Venter, W. A. "Dinizulu en sy Raadgewers. 'n Vroeë Besoek aan die Jong Zoeloekoning," <u>Historia</u>, vol. 9, no. 2 (June 1964), 82-84.

464. Von Sicard, H. "Shaka and the North," <u>AS</u>, vol. 14, no. 4 (1955), 145-54.

465. Wheelwright, C. A. "Native Administration in Zululand," <u>JAS</u>, vol. 24 (1924-25), 92-99.

<u>See also</u>: V, X-B, XV, XVI, XVII, XX, XXI

D. <u>Southern Sotho</u>

466. Ashton, E. H. "Political Organisation of the Southern Sotho," <u>BS</u>, vol. 12, no. 4 (Dec. 1938), 287-320.

467. Dornan, S. S. "The Basuto, Their Traditional History and Folklore," <u>PRSA</u>, vol. 8, no. 1 (1908), 65-94.

468. Fairclough, T. Lindsay. "Notes on the Basuto, Their History, Country, Etc.," JAS, vol. 4 (1904-05), 194-205.

469. Franz, G. H. "The Literature of Lesotho (Basutoland)," BS, vol. 4, no. 3 (Sept. 1930), 145-80.

470. Guillarmod, A. M. "Notes on the Article 'Les Plantes et l'Ethnographie au Basutoland' by F. Laydevant O.M.I.," Annali del Potificio Museo Missionario Etnologico, vol. 29 (1965), 397-414.

471. Guma, S. M. "Some Aspects of Circumcision in Basutoland," AS, vol. 24, no. 3-4 (1965), 241-49.

472. Hamnett, Ian. "Koena Chieftainship Seniority in Basutoland," Africa, vol. 35, no. 3 (July 1965), 241-51.

473. How, M. "An Alibi for Mantatisi," AS, vol. 13, no. 2 (1954), 65-76.

474. Jones, G. I. "Chiefly Succession in Basutoland," in Goody, Jack, ed., Succession to High Office (Cambridge Papers in Social Anthropology 4), (Cambridge, 1966), 57-81.

475. Jousse, T. "Moshesh, Roi des Bassoutos," Le Chrétien Evangélique (Revue Religieuse de la Suisse Romande), 1867.

476. Kruger, F. "Tlokwa Traditions," BS, vol. 11, no. 2 (June 1937), 85-115.

477. Laydevant, F. "Le Sceptre des Chefs Basuto," Africa, vol. 18, no. 1 (Jan. 1948), 41-44.

478. Le Roux, Hannah. "Basutoland," Scottish Geographical Magazine, vol. 56, no. 3 (Nov. 1940), 97-102.

479. Lye, William F. "The Difaqane: The Mfecane in the Southern Sotho Area," JAH, vol. 8, no. 1 (1967), 107-31.

480. Mabille, H. E. "The Basuto of Basutoland," JAS, vol. 5, no. 19 (April 1906), 233-51; vol. 5, no. 20 (July 1906), 351-76.

481. MacGregor, J. C. "Some Notes on the Basuto Tribal System, Political and Social," RSAAAS, vol. 6, no. 7 (1910), 276-81.

482. Norton, Rev. "A Description of the Modderpoort Neighbor-hood One Hundred Years Ago," RSAAAS, vol. 6, no. 3 (1910), 114-17.

483. Norton, W. A. "Sesuto Praises of the Chiefs," RSAAAS, vol. 18, no. 3-4 (1922), 441-53.

484. Perrot, Claude-Hélène. "Une culte messianique chez les Sotho au milieu du XIXe siècle," Archives de Sociologie des Religions, vol. 9, no. 18 (July-Dec. 1964), 147-52.

485. _____. "Premières années de l'implantation du christian-isme au Lesotho (1833-1847)," Cahiers d'Études Africaines, vol. 4, no. 13 (1963), 97-124.

486. Smith, E. W. "Sebetwane and the Makololo," AS, vol. 15, no. 2 (1956), 49-74.

487. Tylden, G. "The Basutoland Rebellion of 1880-81," JSAHR, vol. 15 (1936), 98-107.

See also: IV-C, V, XV, XVIII, XIX, XXI

E. Northern Sotho and Venda

488. Becken, H. J. "The Constitution of the Lutheran Bapedi Church of 1892," Bulletin of the Society for African Church History, vol. 2, no. 2 (1966), 180-89.

489. Bothma, C. V. "Ntšhabeleng Social Structure," EP 48, 94 pp.

490. Bullock, Charles. "Notes on the Ba-Venda," NADA, vol. 4 (1926), 62-66.

491. De Vaal, J. B. "Ysterbewerking deur die Bawenda en die Balemba in Soutpansberg," TWK (New Series), vol. 3, no. 1 (Aug. 1942), 45-50.

492. Du Plessis, H. "Die Territoriale Organisasie van die Venda," AS, vol. 4, no. 3 (Sept. 1945), 122-27.

493. Eiselen, Werner. "Über die Häuptlingswürde bei den Bapedi," Africa, vol. 5, no. 3 (July 1932), 297-306.

494. Grilo, V. H. Velez. "The Dispersion of the 'Wa-remba' (or 'Vha-lemba') and Tribes Related, South of the Zambezi," SAJS, vol. 54, no. 5 (May 1958), 111-16.

495. Hunt, D. R. "An Account of the Bapedi," BS, vol. 5, no. 4 (Dec. 1931), 275-326.

496. Krige, J. D. and E. J. "The Lobedu of the Transvaal," in Forde, D., ed., African Worlds (London, 1954), 55-82.

497. Krige, E. J. "Note on the Phalaborwa and Their Morula Complex," BS, vol. 11, no. 4 (Dec. 1937), 357-66.

498. _____. "The Place of the North-Eastern Transvaal Sotho in the South Bantu Complex," Africa, vol. 11, no. 3 (July 1938), 265-93.

499. Krige, J. D. "The Significance of Cattle Exchanges in Lobedu Social Structure," Africa, vol. 12, no. 4 (Oct. 1939), 393-424.

500. _____. "Traditional Origins and Tribal Relationships of the Sotho of the Northern Transvaal," BS, vol. 11, no. 4 (Dec. 1937), 321-56.

501. Kruger, F. "The Lobedu," BS, vol. 10, no. 1 (March 1936), 89-105.

502. Lestrade, G. P. "Some Notes on the Ethnic History of the Bavenda and Their Rhodesia Affinities," SAJS, vol. 24 (Dec. 1927), 486-95.

503. _____. "Some Notes on the Political Organization of the Venda-Speaking Tribes," Africa, vol. 3, no. 3 (July 1930), 306-22.

504. Lombaard, B. V. "Bydraes tot Bronne oor Johannes Dinkwanyane," Historia, vol. 10, no. 1 (Mar. 1965), 4-15.

505. _____, and C. W. Prinsloo. "Die Voorgeskiedenis en Opkoms van die Bapedi-Stam," HS, vol. 6, no. 4 (Dec. 1945), 213-16.

506. Möller-Malan, Dorothea. "Die Donker Soutpansberg," Historia, vol. 1, no. 3 (Feb. 1957), 219-30; vol. 2, no. 1 (June 1957), 35-50; vol. 2, no. 2 (Sept. 1957), 167-83; vol. 3, no. 1 (Mar. 1958), 47-53; vol. 3, no. 2 (June 1958), 115-21; vol. 3, no. 3 (Sept. 1958), 185-97; vol. 3, no. 4 (Dec. 1958), 256-66.

507. Mönnig, H. O. "The Baroka ba Nkwana," AS, vol. 22, no. 4 (1963), 170-75.

508. _____. "The Structure of Lobedu Social and Political Organisation," AS, vol. 22, no. 2 (1963), 49-64.

509. Otto, J. C. "Oorsake en Gebeurtenisse wat Indirek en Regstreeks Aanleiding gegee het tot die Veldtog teen Sekoekoeni (1876)," HS, vol. 7, no. 4 (Dec. 1946), 148-63.

510. _____. "Sekoekoeni en die Handel in Vuurwapens," HS, vol. 5, no. 3 (Sept. 1944), 161-74.

511. _____. "Die voorgeskiedenis en opkoms van die Bapedi-Stam," HS, vol. 6, no. 2 (June 1945), 73-80.

512. Potgieter, E. F. "Enkele Volksverhale van die Ndzundza van Transvaal," CUSA, C9 (1958), 36 pp.

513. Rademeyer, J. I. "Die Oorlog teen Magato (M'pefu)," HS, vol. 5, no. 2 (June 1944), 79-122.

514. Reuter, F. "Modjadje, A Native Queen in Northern Transvaal: An Ethnological Study," RSAAAS, vol. 3 (1905-06), 242-50.

515. Roberts, Noel. "The Bagananoa or Ma-laboch: Notes on Their Early History, Customs and Creed," RSAAAS, vol. 2 (1915), 241-56.

516. Smith, K. W. "The Fall of the Bapedi of the North-Eastern Transvaal," JAH, vol. 10, no. 2 (1969), 237-52.

517. Stayt, H. A. "Notes on the Ba Lemba," JRAI, vol. 61 (1931), 231-38.

518. Thompson, Louis C. "The Balemba of Southern Rhodesia," NADA, vol. 19 (1942), 76-86.

519. Tylden, G. "The Sekukuni Campaign of November-December 1879," JSAHR, vol. 29 (1951), 128-36.

520. Van Coller, H. P. "Mampoer in die Stryd om die Bapedi-Troon (Die Mapochoorlog 1882-1883)," HS, vol. 3, no. 3-4 (Oct.-Dec. 1942), 97-152.

521. Van Warmelo, N. J. "The Bahwaduba," EP 19, pp. 23-32.

522. _____. "The Bakgatla ba ga Mosêtlha," EP 17, pp. 3-11.

523. _____. "The Bakoni ba Maake," EP 12, pp. 19-25.

524. _____. "The Bakoni of Mametša," EP 15, pp. 41-48.

525. _____. "The Ba Letswalô or Banarene," EP 10, pp. 3-11.

526. _____. "The Banarene of Mmutlana," EP 14, pp. 37-39.

527. _____. "The Banarene of Sekôrôrô," EP 13, pp. 27-35.

528. _____. "The Bathlabine of Moxobôya," EP 11, pp. 13-18.

529. _____. "The Batubatse of Mašišmale," EP 16, pp. 49-53.

530. _____. "Contributions towards Venda History, Religion and Tribal Ritual," EP 3, 207 pp.

531. _____. "Copperminers of Messina and the Early History of Zoutpansberg," EP 8, 209 pp.

532. _____. "A Genealogy of the House of Sekhukhune," EP 21, pp. 45-55.

533. _____. "History of Ha Makuya," EP 22, pp. 57-65.

534. _____. "Die Tlokwa en Birwa van Noord Transvaal," EP 29, 86 pp.

535. Van Zyl, H. J. "Praises in Northern Sotho," BS, vol. 15, no. 2 (June 1941), 119-56.

536. Von Sicard, H. "Lemba Clans," NADA, vol. 39 (1962), 68-80.

537. _____. "Lemba Initiation Chants," Ethnos, vol. 28, no. 2-4 (1963), 198-209.

538. _____. "Mambo Dyembewu," PTRSA, vol. 43 (May 1951), 175-215.

539. Winter, J. A. "The History of Sekwati," RSAAAS, vol. 9 (1912), 329-32.

540. Winter, J. A. "Hymns in Praise of Famous Chiefs," RSAAAS, vol. 9 (1912), 377-82.

541. _____. The Tradition of Ra'lolo (Induna of Sekukuni II)," RSAAAS, vol. 9 (1912), 87-100.

    See also: X-C, XX

F. Western Sotho (Tswana)

542. Ashton, E. H. "Notes on the Political and Judicial Organisation of the Tswana," BS, vol. 11, no. 2 (June 1937), 67-83.

543. Breutz, P. L. "Die Stamme van die Distrikte Lichtenburg en Delareyville," EP 37, 135 pp.

544. _____. "Die Stamme van die Distrik Ventersdorp," EP 31, 152 pp.

545. _____. "The Tribes of the Districts of Kuruman and Postmasburg," EP 49, 258 pp.

546. _____. "The Tribes of Mafeking District," EP 32, 315 pp.

547. _____. "The Tribes of Marico District," EP 30, 266 pp.

548. _____. "Tribes of Rustenburg and Pilansberg Districts," EP 28, 501 pp.

549. _____. "The Tribes of Vryburg District," EP 46, 207 pp.

550. Ellenberger, V. "History of the Batlôkwa of Gaberones (Bechuanaland Protectorate)," BS, vol. 13, no. 3 (Sept. 1939), 165-98.

551. _____. "Di Rōbarōba Matlhakola-Tsa Ga Masodi-a-Mphela," TRSSA, vol. 25, no. 1 (1937-38), 1-72.

552. Fredoux, F. "Quelques Mots sur les Bechuanas," Géographie, series 4, no. 14 (1857), 369-83.

553. Language, F. J. "Die Bogwera van die Tlhaping," TWK (New Series), vol. 4, no. 2 (Dec. 1943), 110-34.

554. Language, F. J. "Herkoms en Geskiedenis van die Tlhaping," AS, vol. 1, no. 2 (1942), 115-34.

555. _____. "Die Verkryging en Verlies van Lidmaatskap tot die Stam by die Tlhaping," AS, vol. 2, no. 2 (June 1943), 77-92.

556. Lestrade, G. P. "Some Notes on the Political Organisation of the Bechwana," SAJS, vol. 25 (Dec. 1928), 427-32.

557. Maingard, L. F. "The Brikwa and the Ethnic Origins of the Batlhaping," SAJS, vol. 30 (Oct. 1933), 597-602.

558. Matthews, Z. K. "A Short History of the Tshidi Barolong," Fort Hare Papers, vol. 1, no. 1 (1945), 9-28.

559. Nettleton, G. E. "History of the Ngamiland Tribes up to 1926," BS, vol. 8, no. 4 (Dec. 1934), 343-60.

560. Pauw, B. A. "Some Changes in the Social Structure of the Tlhaping of the Taung Reserve," AS, vol. 19, no. 2 (1960), 49-76.

561. Rust, H. J. "Was Uns Ein Altes Schriftstück Erzählt," JSWASS, vol. 15 (1960-61), 47-55.

562. Saunders, C. C. "Early Knowledge of the Sotho: Seventeenth and Eighteenth Century Accounts of the Tswana," QBSAL, vol. 20, no. 3 (March 1966), 60-70.

563. Schapera, I. "The BaKxatla BaxaKxafêla. Preliminary Report of Field Investigations," Africa, vol. 6, no. 4 (Oct. 1933), 402-14.

564. _____. "Christianity and the Tswana," JRAI, vol. 88, pt. 1 (Jan.-June 1958), 1-9.

565. _____. "The Contributions of Western Civilization to Modern Kxatla Culture," TRSSA, vol. 24, no. 3 (1937), 221-52.

566. _____. "Ethnographic Texts in the Boloongwe Dialect of Sekgalagadi," BS, vol. 12, no. 3 (Sept. 1938), 157-88.

567. _____. "Kinship and Politics in Tswana History," JRAI, vol. 93, pt. 2 (July-Dec. 1963), 159-73.

568.   Schapera, I. "Notes on the History of the Kaa," AS, vol. 4, no. 3 (Sept. 1945), 109-21.

569.   _____, and D. F. Van der Merwe. "Notes on the Tribal Groupings, History, and Customs of the Bakgalagadi," SAS-UCT (New Series), no. 13 (Sept. 1945), 193 pp.

570.   _____. "The Political Annals of a Tswana Tribe," SAS-UCT (New Series), no. 18 (Nov. 1947), 132 pp.

571.   _____. "The Political Organization of the Ngwato of Bechuana-land Protectorate," in Fortes, M., and E. E. Evans-Pritchard, eds., African Political Systems (London, 1940), 56-82.

572.   _____. "The Social Structure of a Tswana Ward," BS, vol. 9, no. 3 (Sept. 1935), 203-24.

573.   _____. "A Short History of the Bakgatla-BagaKgafêla of Bechuanaland Protectorate," SAS-UCT (New Series), no. 3 (July 1942), 54 pp.

574.   _____. "A Short History of the Bangwaketse," AS, vol. 1, no. 1 (1942), 1-26.

575.   _____. "Tribal Courts in the Bechuanaland Protectorate," AS, vol. 2, no. 1 (Mar. 1943), 27-40.

576.   Silberbauer, G. B., and A. J. Kuper. "Kgalagari Masters and Bushmen Serfs: Some Observations," AS, vol. 25, no. 4 (1966), 171-79.

577.   Stigand, A. G. "Notes on N'Gamiland," TRSSA, vol. 3, no. 3 (1913), 379-91.

578.   Van Niekerk, B. J. "Notes on the Administration of Justice among the Kwena," AS, vol. 25, no. 1 (1966), 37-45.

579.   Van Warmelo, N. J. "The Tribes of Vryburg District," EP 20, pp. 33-43.

580.   Von Sicard, H. "Rhodesian Sidelights on Bechuanaland History," NADA, vol. 31 (1954), 67-94.

See also: V, XXI

G. Ndebele

581. Brown, Richard. "The Ndebele Succession Crisis 1868-1877," in Leverhulme Inter-Collegiate History Conference, Proceedings, Historians in Tropical Africa (University College of Rhodesia and Nyasaland, Salisbury, 1962), pp. 159-75.

582. Carbutt, C. L. "A Brief Account of the Rise and Fall of the Matabele," NADA, vol. 25 (1948), 38-44.

583. Carnegie, D. "Lobengula and His People," PRSA, vol. 6, no. 2 (1906), 111-17.

584. Carnegie, W. A. "Brief Notes on Lobengula and His People," NADA, vol. 11 (1933), 13-22.

585. Cooper-Chadwick, J. and A. Boggie. "Correspondence on Mr. H. Marshall Hole's Paper on the Rise of the Matabele," PRSA, vol. 13, no. 1 (1913-14), 5-9.

586. E.H.B. "Notes on the Matabele Occupation of Southern Rhodesia," NADA, vol. 13 (1935), 14-17.

587. Gambo, Frank. "Some True History about the Royal House of the 'Gambos'," NADA, vol. 39 (1962), 46-51.

588. H.M.G.J. "A Sketch of Lobengula," NADA, vol. 10 (1932), 39-44.

589. Hole, H. Marshall. "The Rise of the Matabele," PRSA, vol. 12, no. 3 (1913), 135-51.

590. Hughes, A.J.B. and Summers, Roger. "The Matabele Warrior: His Arms and Accoutrements," Occ. Pap. Nat. Mus. S. Rhod., vol. 2, no. 20 (Nov. 1955), 779-91.

591. Kendal, Father J., ed. "Father Hartmann's Notes," NADA, vol. 22 (1945), 10-18.

592. Kendal, Father J. "Getting Across," NADA, vol. 15 (1938), 40-43.

593. Kotzé, D. J. "Die Eerste Amerikaanse Sendelinge onder die Matabeles," AYB, pt. 1 (1950), 129-318.

594. Lewis, D. G. "The Battle of Zwangendaba," NADA, vol. 33 (1956), 51-52.

595.   Lye, William F. "The Ndebele Kingdom South of the Limpopo River," JAH, vol. 10, no. 1 (1969), 87-104.

596.   Ncube, R.M.M. "The True Story re Chaminuka and Lobengula," NADA, vol. 39 (1962), 59-67.

597.   O'Neil, Rev. "The Natives of South-West Matabeleland and Some of Their Religious Customs," PRSA, vol. 19 (1920-21), 3-11.

598.   Pitout, J. A. "The Arrival of the Mandebele in Rhodesia as Told by Siatsha," NADA, vol. 30 (1953), 57-58.

599.   _____. "Lobengula's Flight and the Shangani Battle as Related by Siatsha--an Eye Witness of the Battle," NADA, vol. 40 (1963), 69-73.

600.   Posselt, F.W.T. "Mzilikzai. The Rise of the Amandebele," PRSA, vol. 18, no. 1 (1920), 3-22.

601.   _____. "Nkulumana. The Disputed Succession. A Chapter of Amandebele History," NADA, vol. 1 (1923), 29-42.

602.   Rademeyer, J. I. "Die Implikasies i.v.m. 'n Opvolger vir Moselekatse as Matabele-Opperhoof," HS, vol. 9, no. 3-4 (April 1949), 66-70.

603.   Summers, Roger. "The Military Doctrine of the Matabele," NADA, vol. 32 (1955), 7-15.

604.   Taylor, G. A. "The Matabele Head Ring (Isidhlodhlo) and Some Fragments of History (Illustrated)," NADA, vol. 3 (1925), 37-42.

605.   Taylor, H. J. "The Amandebele, and Other Tribes of Matabeleland," PRSA, vol. 6, no. 1 (1906), 22-32.

606.   Van Warmelo, N. J. "The Ndebele of J. Kekana," EP 18, 13-21.

607.   _____. "Transvaal Ndebele Texts," EP 1, 108 pp.

608.   Wallis, J.P.R. "Southern Rhodesian Government Archives. The Oppenheimer Series," NADA, vol. 23 (1946), 72-74.

609.   Woods, G.G.B. "Extracts from Customs and History; Amandebele," NADA, vol. 9 (1931), 16-23.

610. Woods, G.G.B. "Matabele History and Customs," <u>NADA</u>, vol. 7 (1929), 43-49.

See also: VI, X-H, XXIII

H. <u>Shona</u>

611. Abraham, D. P. "The Early Political History of the Kingdom of Mwene Mutapa (850-1589)," in Leverhulme Inter-Collegiate History Conference, Proceedings. <u>Historians in Tropical Africa</u> (University College of Rhodesia and Nyasaland, Salisbury, 1962), pp. 61-92.

612. _____. "Ethno-History of the Empire of Mutapa. Problems and Methods," in Vansina, J., L. V. Thomas, and R. Mauny, eds., <u>The Historian in Tropical Africa</u> (London, 1964), 104-26.

613. _____. "Maramuca: An Exercise in the Combined Use of Portuguese Records and Oral Tradition," <u>JAH</u>, vol. 2, no. 2 (1961), 211-25.

614. _____. "The Monomotapa Dynasty," <u>NADA</u>, vol. 36 (1959), 58-84.

615. _____. "The Principality of Maungwe: Its History and Traditions," <u>NADA</u>, vol. 28 (1951), 56-83.

616. _____. "The Roles of 'Chaminuka' and the Mhondoro-Cults in Shona Political History," in Stokes, E. and R. Brown, eds., <u>The Zambesian Past</u> (Manchester, 1966), 28-46.

617. Baker, Robert H. "The Mutasa and Makoni Dynasties," <u>NADA</u>, vol. 2 (1924), 85-87.

618. Blake-Thompson, J., and Roger Summers. "Mlimo and Mwari: Notes on a Native Religion in Southern Rhodesia," <u>NADA</u>, vol. 33 (1956), 53-58.

619. Chidziwa, Joshua. "History of the Vashawasha," <u>NADA</u> (New Series), vol. 9, no. 1 (1964), 16-33.

620. Chieza, G. P. "The History of Chieza and his Red Dangers (In English and Chizezuru)," <u>NADA</u>, vol. 18 (1941), 52-68.

621. Devlin, Christopher. "The Mashona and the British," <u>Month</u> (New Series), vol. 25, no. 4 (April 1961), 197-208.

622. Devlin, Christopher. "The Mashona and the Portuguese," Month (New Series), vol. 25, no. 3 (March 1961), 140-51.

623. Deyo, Marguerite. "History of the Mutambara Tribe," NADA, vol. 32 (1955), 55-64.

624. Edwards, William. "From Birth to Death. Notes on the Natives of the Mrewa District, Southern Rhodesia," NADA, vol. 7 (1929), 16-42.

625. _____. "The Wanoe: A Short Historical Sketch," NADA, vol. 4 (1926), 13-28.

626. Fortune, G. "Ndevo Yengombe Luvizho and Other Lilima Texts," SAS-UCT (New Series), no. 21 (July 1949), 86 pp.

627. Franklin, H. "Nyaningwe. Notes on the Chibi Family," NADA, vol. 6 (1928), 80-87.

628. Garbett, G. Kingsley. "Prestige, Status, and Power in a Modern Valley Korekore Chiefdom, Rhodesia," Africa, vol. 37, no. 3 (July 1967), 307-26.

629. Hannan, Father. "The Kutama Lineage," NADA, vol. 39 (1962), 55-58.

630. Hemans, H. N. "History of the Abenanzwa Tribe," PRSA, vol. 12, no. 2 (1912), 85-112.

631. Honyera. "The Story of the Masunda Headmanship," NADA (New Series), vol. 9, no. 1 (1964), 55-59.

632. Hove, M. M. "Notes on the Vangowa Tribe," NADA, vol. 20 (1943), 41-45.

633. Howman, E. G. "The Traditional History and Customs of the Makaranga (Warozwi)," RSAAAS, vol. 15, no. 6 (March-April 1919), 383-93.

634. "Mafohla." "The Curse of Chigodoro. An Incident in the History of the Vambire Tribe," NADA, vol. 6 (1928), 20-23.

635. Marconnes, Francisque. "The Karangas," NADA, vol. 10 (1932), 11-18.

636. Marconnes, Francisque. "The Rozvis, or Destroyers," NADA, vol. 11 (1933), 72-90.

637. Marodzi. "The Barozwi," NADA, vol. 2 (1924), 88-91.

638. Martin, C. "Manyika Beads of the XIXth Century," NADA, vol. 17 (1940), 18-26.

639. Mauch, Karl (tr. F. O. Bernhard, notes by M. Gelfand). "The Makalaka," Rhodesiana, vol. 12 (Sept. 1965), 63-75.

640. Meredith, L. C. "The Rain Spirit of Mabota Murangadzwa," NADA, vol. 3 (1925), 77-81.

641. Morris, S. E. "The Origin of Some Mashona Names of Chiefs and Places," NADA, vol. 10 (1932), 18-20.

642. Muhlanga, S. "In the Early Days," NADA, vol. 4 (1926), 107-10.

643. _____. "Mbava and Others," NADA, vol. 4 (1926), 91-93.

644. Nobbs, E. A. "The Native Cattle of Southern Rhodesia," SAJS, vol. 24 (Dec. 1927), 328-42.

645. Posselt, F.W.T. "Marondera," NADA, vol. 5 (1927), 47-48.

646. _____. "Social Conditions of the Natives of Mashonaland," PRSA, vol. 12, no. 3 (1913), 119-34.

647. _____. "The Watawara and the Batonga," NADA, vol. 7, (1929), 80-95.

648. Robinson, K. R. "A History of the Bikita District," NADA, vol. 34 (1957), 75-87.

649. Seed, J. H. "A Glimpse of Native History. The Vashawasha," NADA, vol. 14 (1936-37), 5-16.

650. _____. "The Kinship System of a Bantu Tribe," NADA, vol. 10 (1932), 65-73; vol. 11 (1933), 35-56.

651. Seymour, Lindsay F. "The Tradition of the VaMare of Chibi," NADA, vol. 17 (1940), 73-76.

652. Smith, H. Stanford. "Monomotapas—A King-list," NADA, vol. 35 (1958), 84-86.

653. Stead, W. H. "The People of Early Rhodesia," PTRSA, vol. 42 (Mar. 1949), 75-83.

654. Taberer, W. S. "Mashonaland Natives," JAS, vol. 4 (1904-5), 311-36.

655. Tagwireyi, Johnson H. "Origin of the Vamari Clan," NADA, vol. 27 (1950), 63-66.

656. Tapson, R. R. "Some Notes on the Mrozwi Occupation of the Sebungwe district," NADA, vol. 21 (1944), 29-32.

657. Tizirai, Paskari. "The Story of the Chilimanzi People," NADA, vol. 26 (1949), 36-38.

658. Van der Merwe, D. J. "Some History of the Vakaranga in the Gutu Reserve," NADA, vol. 14 (1936-37), 71-74.

659. Von Sicard, Harald. "The Origin of Some of the Tribes in the Belingwe Reserve," NADA, vol. 25 (1948), 93-104; vol. 27 (1950), 7-19; vol. 28 (1951), 5-25; vol. 29 (1952), 43-64; vol. 30 (1953), 64-71; vol. 32 (1955), 77-92.

660. _____. "Reiche und Königtum der Rozwi vom Ende des 17 biz sum Anfang des 19 Jahrhunderts," in Haberland, E., M. Schuster, and H. Straube, eds., Festschrift für Ad. E. Jensen (Munich, 1964), pt. II, pp. 635-63.

See also: IV-F, X-G, XXIII

I. The Bantu-Speaking Peoples of South-West Africa

661. Abel, Herbert. "Völkerkundlich-kulturgeographische Beobach-tungen in Südwestafrika und Südangola (1952-1957)," Veröff Ubersee-Museum, Bremen (Series B), vol. 1, no. 3 (1959), 165-87.

662. Hahn, C.H.L. "Preliminary Notes on Certain Customs of the Ovambo," JSWASS, vol. 3 (1927-28), 5-33.

663. Köhler, O. "A Study of Gobabis District (South West Africa)," EP 42, 103 pp.

664. _____. "A Study of Grootfontein District (South West Africa)," EP 45, 85 pp.

665. Köhler, O. "A Study of Karibib District (South West Africa),"
EP 40, 116 pp.

666. _____. "A Study of Omaruṟu District (South West Africa),"
EP 43, 113 pp.

667. _____. "A Study of Otjiwarongo District (South West Africa),"
EP 44, 98 pp.

668. Larson, Thomas J. "The Significance of Rainmaking for the
Mbukushu," AS, vol. 25, no. 1 (1966), 23-36.

669. Schapera, I. "Notes on Some Herero Genealogies," SAS-UCT
(New Series), no. 14 (Oct. 1945), 39 pp.

670. Seymour, John. "Hunters, Herders, and Farmers in South-
West Africa," The Geographical Magazine, vol. 23, no. 10
(Feb. 1951), 470-82.

671. Van Warmelo, N. J. "Notes on the Kaokoveld (South West
Africa) and its People," EP 26, pp. 1-64.

672. Vedder, H. "Maharero und seine Zeit im Lichte der Doku-
mente seines Nachlasses," JSWASS, vol. 5 (1929-31), 5-31.

673. Wagner, Günter. "A Study of Okahandja District (South West
Africa)," EP 38, 106 pp.

674. Wilhelm, Joachim H. "Die Hukwe," Stadtisches Museums für
Völkerkunde Jahrbuch (Leipzig), vol. 13 (1954-55), 8-44.

See also: VII, VIII

J. The Bantu-Speaking Peoples of Moçambique

675. Almeida, A. "Os Estados Antigos dos Nativos de Moçambique
(Sul do Rio Save) Quanto à Liberdade," Moçambique (Lisboa,
1965), 97-119.

676. Earthy, E. Dora. "Sundry Notes on the Vandau of Sofala,
P.E.A.," BS, vol. 4, no. 2 (June 1930), 95-107.

677. Junod, H. P. "Notes on the Ethnological Situation in Portuguese
East Africa in the South of the Zambesi," BS, vol. 10, no. 3
(Sept. 1936), 293-312.

678. Rita-Ferreira, A. "Mozambique Ethnic Characterization and Grouping," <u>SAJS,</u> vol. 55, no. 8 (Aug. 1959), 201-4.

679. Travassos dos Santos Dias, J. A. "The Status of the Tsetse Fly in Mozambique before 1896," <u>SAJS</u>, vol. 58 (1962), 243-47.

680. Warhurst, P. R. "The Scramble and African Politics in Gaza-land," in Stokes, E., and R. Brown, eds., <u>The Zambesian Past</u> (Manchester, 1966), pp. 47-62.

<u>See also:</u> VI

XI   ALIEN VISITORS IN SOUTHERN AFRICA BEFORE 1652

681. Burton, R., and E. Terry. "A View of the Bay of Souldania," <u>QBSAL</u>, vol. 1, no. 3 (1946-47), 71-77.

682. Jeffreys, M.D.W. "Arabs and the Discovery of the Cape," <u>ANN</u>, vol. 13, no. 6 (June 1959), 237-40.

683. Mackenzie, Norman H. "Captain Cross and the First English Settlement at the Cape," <u>QBSAL</u>, vol. 2, no. 1 (Sept. 1947), 3-17; vol. 2, no. 2 (Dec. 1947), 49-54.

684. Raven-Hart, R., tr. "Travels, 1644-1653. Johann Jacob Merklein," <u>ANN</u>, vol. 16, no. 3 (Sept. 1964), 108-13.

685. Rochlin, S. A. "Early Arab Knowledge of the Cape of Good Hope," <u>ANN</u>, vol. 13, no. 1 (Mar. 1958), 32-47.

686. Schapera, Isaac. "The First Attempt at European Settlement of the Cape," <u>South African Quarterly</u>, vol. 5, no. 3 (Sept.-Nov. 1923), 13-16.

<u>See also:</u> XII

XII   THE PORTUGUESE IN SOUTHERN AFRICA

687. Axelson, Eric. "Beacons of Portuguese Discovery," <u>Historia</u>, vol. 1, no. 3 (Feb. 1957), 231-38.

688. _____. "Finding of a Bartolomeu Dias Beacon," <u>SAGJ</u>, vol. 21 (April 1939), 28-38.

689. Axelson, Eric. "Portuguese Settlement in the Interior of South-East Africa in the Seventeenth Century," Congresso Internacional de História dos Descobrimentos, Actas 5, pt. 2 (1961), 1-17.

690. Ford, E. B. "Some Points Connected with the Discovery of the Cape by Bartholomeu Dias, 1488," RSAAAS, vol. 16, no. 4 (1920), 354-64.

691. Godlonton, W. A. "The Journeys of Antonio Fernandes—The First Known European to Find the Monomotapa and to Enter Southern Rhodesia," PTRSA, vol. 40 (April 1945), 71-103.

692. _____. "Journeys of Antonio Fernandes—Some Amendments," PTRSA, vol. 48 (August 1960), 44-48.

693. Hole, H. Marshall, "Portuguese Exploration in Southern Rhodesia," PRSA, vol. 6, no. 2 (1906), 91-102.

694. Newitt, M. D. D. "The Portuguese on the Zambezi: An Historical Interpretation of the Prazo System," JAH, vol. 10, no. 1 (1969), 67-85.

695. Price, T. "Portuguese Relations with David Livingstone," The Scottish Geographical Magazine, vol. 71, no. 3 (Dec. 1955), 138-46.

696. Rea, W. F. "[The Life of Gonçalo da Silveira 1526-1560]," Rhodesiana, vol. 6 (1961), 1-40.

697. Schofield, J. F. "The Journeys of Antonio Fernandes—Some Footnotes," PTRSA, vol. 42 (Mar. 1949), 84-95.

698. Seruya, Salomon. "History of Early Portuguese Discoveries and Exploration in Africa," RSAAAS, vol. 10 (1913), 67-80.

699. Silva Rego, A. da. "Portuguese Contributions to the Ethnological and Geographical Knowledge of Africa during the XVIth Century," SAJS, vol. 49, no. 3-4 (Oct.-Nov. 1952), 93-103.

700. _____. "Relaçoes entre Moçambique e a Africa do sul (1652-1900)," Moçambique (Lisboa, 1965), 57-76.

See also: X-E, X-H, X-J, XX

701. Anders, H. D. "Marginal Notes to Wikar's Journal (Van Rie-beeck Society XV, 1935," BS, vol. 11, no. 1 (Mar. 1937), 47-52.

702. Anon. "The Origin and Incidence of Miscegenation at the Cape during the Dutch East India Company's Regime, 1652-1795," Race Relations Journal, vol. 20, no. 2 (1953), 23-27.

703. Blommaert, W. "Het invoeren van de Slavernij aan de Kaap," AYB, pt. 1 (1938), 1-29.

704. Böeseken, A. J. "Die Nederlandse Kommissarisse en die 18de Eeuse Samelewing aan die Kaap," AYB (1944), 1-253.

705. Bokhorst, M. "Die Waldense en Suid-Afrika," HS, vol. 1, no. 2 (Oct. 1939), 1-4.

706. Bosman, D. B. "Afrikaanse Taaltoestande tydens Jan van Riebeek," TWK, vol. 1 (1922-23), 4-17.

707. _____. "Oor die Afkoms van die Boere," TWK, vol. 1 (1922-23), 206-14.

708. _____. "Die Outeurskap van die Kaapse Dagverhaal in die Tyd van van Riebeeck," Hertzog-Annale, vol. 2 (Dec. 1955), 12-28.

709. Bosman, F. C. L. "Die Invloed van die Hugenote op die Afri-kaanse Volkskarakter en Kultuur," HS, vol. 1, no. 3 (Jan. 1940), 1-14.

710. Botha, C. Graham. "Criminal Procedure at the Cape during the Seventeenth and Eighteenth Centuries," SALJ, vol. 32, pt. 4 (1915), 319-27.

711. _____. "The Dispersion of the Stock Farmer in Cape Colony in the Eighteenth Century," RSAAAS, vol. 20, no. 2 (Dec. 1923), 574-80.

712. _____. "Early Cape Land Tenure," SALJ, vol. 36, pt. 2 (1919), 149-60; vol. 36, pt. 3, 225-33.

713. _____. "Early Cape Matrimonial Law," SALJ, vol. 31, pt. 3 (1914), 250-60.

714. Botha, C. Graham. "Huguenots in South Africa," Proceedings of the Huguenot Society of London, vol. 13, no. 6 (1929), 579-90.

715. _____. "The Early History of the Cape Province, as Illustrated by Dutch Place Names," RSAAAS, vol. 19 (1922), 433-38.

716. _____. "The Early Inferior Courts of Justice at the Cape," SALJ, vol. 38, pt. 4 (1921), 406-23.

717. _____. "Early Legal Practitioners of the Cape Colony," SALJ, vol. 41, pt. 3 (1924), 255-62.

718. _____. "The Public Prosecutor of the Cape Colony up to 1828," SALJ, vol. 35, pt. 4 (1918), 399-406.

719. _____. "Slavery at the Cape," SALJ, vol. 50 (1933), 4-12.

720. Boxer, C. R. "The Tavern of Two Seas. The Cape of Good Hope under the Dutch East India Company, 1652-1795," History Today, vol. 14, pt. 1 (June 1964), 391-98.

721. Coetzee, C. G. "Die Kompanjie se besetting van Delagoabaai," AYB, pt. 2 (1948), 167-276.

722. Coetzee, N. A. "Jacobus Coetsee: Die Boerepionier van Groot-Namakwaland," Historia, vol. 3, no. 3 (Sept. 1958), 169-77.

723. Coolhaas, W. Ph. "De Carrière van Jan van Riebeeck," Historia, vol. 11, no. 1 (Mar. 1966), 18-35.

724. _____. "Gegevens Over de Vestiging aan de Kaap de Goede Hoop uit de Generale Missiven," Historia, vol. 7, no. 2 (June 1962), 95-105; vol. 11, no. 3 (Sept. 1966), 191-201.

725. David, Percival. "Proot of Janszen and Proot: A Foot-note to the Early History of the Cape," ANN, vol. 1, no. 2 (Mar. 1944), 3-9.

726. Denoon, G. "The Development of Methods of Land Registration in South Africa," SALJ, vol. 61, no. 1 (Feb. 1944), 4-13.

727. Du Plessis, A. J. "Die Geskiedenis van die Graankultuur in Suid-Afrika, 1652-1752," Stellenbosch B., vol. 11, no. 1 (Sept. 1933), 1-127.

728. Forbes, Vernon S. "Cloppenburg's Journey, 1768," ANN, vol. 15, no. 3 (Sept. 1962), 113-22.

729. Franken, J.L.M. "Huisonderwys aan die Kaap (1692-1732)," Stellenbosch B., vol. 12, no. 1a (July 1934), 1-23.

730. _____. " 'n Kaapse Huishoue in die 18de Eeu uit von Dessin se Briefboek en Memoriaal," AYB, pt. 1 (1940), 1-88.

731. Geyer, A. L. "Die Stellenbosse Gemeente in die Agtiende Eeu," Stellenbosch B., vol. 4, no. 1 (June 1926), 1-99.

732. Gie, S. F. N. "Stages in our Economic History under the Dutch East India Company," RSAAAS, vol. 21 (Nov. 1924), 643-50.

733. Godée-Molsbergen, E. C. "Some Remarks on the White Population at the Cape before the Arrival of the Huguenots," RSAAAS, vol. 5 (1908), 394-401.

734. Goiran, Henri. "L'installation des Huguenots français dans la colonie du Cap," Revue des Sciences Politiques, vol. 51 (July-Sept. 1928), 411-32.

735. Hall, C. G. "The Origin of Water Rights in South Africa," SALJ, vol. 54, pt. 2 (May 1937), 160-72.

736. Hinde, W. H. "The Huguenot Settlement at the Cape of Good Hope," Proceedings of the Huguenot Society of London, vol. 5, no. 2 (1894-95), 205-21.

737. Hoge, J. "Privaatskoolmeesters aan die Kaap in die 18de Eeu," Stellenbosch B., vol. 12, no. 1b (July 1934), 7-59; vol. 15, no. 2 (June 1937), 1-27.

738. _____. "Die Geskiedenis van die Lutherse Kerk aan die Kaap," AYB, pt. 2 (1938), 1-243.

739. _____. "Personalia of the Germans at the Cape, 1652-1806," AYB (1946), 1-495.

740. _____. "Verbeterings en Aanvullings op die 'Geslacht-Register der Oude Kaapsche Familiën'," HS, vol. 8, no. 2 (Jan. 1948), 61-84; vol. 8, no. 3-4 (April 1948), 138-74; vol. 9, no. 1-2 (Aug. 1948), 40-56; vol. 9, no. 3-4 (April 1949), 78-93.

741. Immelman, R. F. M. "The Meuron Regiment at the Cape. First Phase, 1781-84. A Preliminary Sketch," Historia, vol. 7, no. 1 (March 1962), 13-30.

742. Kirby, Percival R. "New Light on the Wreck of the 'Grosvenor' East Indiaman, 1782," ANN, vol. 2, no. 3 (June 1945), 65-92; vol. 2, no. 4 (Sept. 1945), 103-19.

743. Koeman, Ir. C. "Landgiften uit de Eerste Helft van die XVIIIe eeuw op een manuscriptkaart uit het Archief der V.O.C.," AYB, pt. 2 (1955), 255-67.

744. Maingard, L. F. "Hendrik Jacob Wikar: His Editors, Translators, and Commentators," BS, vol. 10, no. 1 (March 1936), 31-40.

745. Marais, M. M. "Armesorg aan die Kaap onder die Kompanjie, 1652-1795," AYB, (1943), 1-72.

746. Muller, C. F. S. "Die Geskiedenis van die vissery aan die Kaap tot aan die middel van die Agtiende Eeu," AYB, pt. 1 (1942), 1-100.

747. Naude, S. D. "Willem Cornelis Boers," AYB, pt. 2 (1950), 355-449.

748. Ploeger, Jan. "Oor die Nederlandse Skeepvaart aan die Kaap en die Landreis van Jacobus Groenendaal," Hertzog-Annale, vol. 7 (Dec. 1960), 48-69.

749. Raum, O. F. "Field Chaplain with the Württemberg Regiment at the Cape, 1788-90," QBSAL, vol. 20, no. 4 (June 1966), 117-31.

750. Raven-Hart, R., tr. "The East-Indian Mirror of Nicholaus de Graaff, 1701," QBSAL, vol. 18, no. 3 (Mar. 1964), 119-34; vol. 18, no. 4 (June 1964), 167-82.

751. _____. "Johan Jacob Saar's Fifteen Years' Military Service, 1662," QBSAL, vol. 20, no. 1 (Sept. 1965), 10-19.

752. Robertson, H. M. "The Economic Development of the Cape under van Riebeeck," SAJE, vol. 13, no. 1 (March 1945), 1-17; vol. 13, no. 2 (June 1945), 75-90; vol. 13, no. 3 (Sept. 1945), 170-84; vol. 13, no. 4 (Dec. 1945), 245-62.

753. Robertson, H. M. "A Further Note on Early Land Tenure at the Cape," SAJE, vol. 12, no. 2 (June 1944), 144-46.

754. _____. "Jan van Riebeeck and His Settlement," SAJE, vol. 20, no. 4 (Dec. 1952), 309-30.

755. _____. "The Politico-Economic Background of Jan van Riebeeck's Settlement," SAJE, vol. 20, no. 3 (Sept. 1952), 205-19.

756. _____. "Some Doubts Concerning Early Land Tenure at the Cape," SAJE, vol. 3, no. 2 (June 1935), 158-72.

757. Roos, J. de V. "The Plakaat Books of the Cape," Cape Law Journal, vol. 14 (1897), 1-23.

758. _____. "The Statute Law of the Cape in Pre-British Days, and Some Judicial Decisions in Relation Thereto," SALJ, vol. 23, pt. 3 (1906), 242-54.

759. Rutherford, G. "Sidelights on Commodore Johnstone's Expedition to the Cape," Mariner's Mirror, vol. 28, no. 3 (July 1942), 189-212; vol. 28, no. 4 (Oct. 1942), 290-308.

760. Scholtz, P. L. "Die Historiese Ontwikkeling van die Onder-Olifantsrivier 1660-1902 ('n Geskiedenis van die Distrik Vanrhynsdorp)," AYB, pt. 2 (1966), 1-212.

761. Smith, A. H. "Wolraad Woltemade and the Wreck of the 'Jonge Thomas'," ANN, vol. 7, no. 1 (Dec. 1949), 2-34.

762. Spilhaus, M. Whiting. "They Planted the Cape," Historia, vol. 11, no. 1 (Mar. 1966), 40-54; vol. 11, no. 2, 125-38; vol. 11, no. 3, 202-14.

763. Stock, J. L. W. "The New Statutes of India at the Cape," SALJ, vol. 32, pt. 4 (1915), 328-37.

764. Swanepoel, H. L. "Oor die Resepsie van die Romeins-Hollandse Reg in Suid-Afrika," Acta Juridica (1958), 7-26.

765. Tylden, G. "The Development of the Commando System in South Africa, 1715 to 1922," ANN, vol. 13, no. 8 (Dec. 1959), 303-13.

766. Van der Merwe, H.J.J.M. "Die Prioriteit van die Kaapse Teks van Jan van Riebeeck se Daghregister," CUSA, C3 (1958), 20 pp.

767. Van Oordt, L. C. "Die Kaapse Taalargief 10. Een-en-Dertig Afrikaans-Hollandse Briewe uit die Jare 1712-1795, Hoofsaaklik Afkomstig van Veldwagmeesters," TWK (New Series), vol. 16, no. 1 (April 1956), 97-125.

768. Van Rensburg, J.I.J. "Die Geskiedenis van die Wingerdkultuur in Suid-Afrika tydens die Eerste Eeu, 1652-1752," AYB, pt. 2 (1954), vii-96.

769. Van Zyl, C. H. "The Batavian and the Cape Plakaten. An Historical Narrative," SALJ, vol. 24, pt. 2 (1907), 132-47; vol. 24, pt. 3, 241-58; vol. 24, pt 4, 366-83; vol. 25, pt. 1 (1908), 4-25; vol. 25, pt. 2, 128-47; vol. 25, pt. 3, 246-66.

770. Venter, P. J. "Landdros en Heemrade (1682-1827)," AYB, pt. 2 (1940), 1-242.

771. Visagie, G. G. "Die Regsbedeling aan die Kaap onder die V.O.C.," Acta Juridica (1963), 118-69.

See also: VI, VIII, XI

XIV   THE CAPE COLONY, 1795-1854

772. Anon. "The Order Book of Captain Augustus Brine, R.N., 1797-1815," QBSAL, vol. 17, no. 3 (March 1963), 75-86; vol. 18, no. 1 (Sept. 1963), 17-26.

773. Arkin, Marcus. "Agency and Island. John Company and the Twilight Years of the Cape—St. Helena Trade, 1822-1836," AYB, pt. 1 (1965), 265-324.

774. _____. "John Company at the Cape. A History of the Agency under Pringle (1794-1815), based on a Study of the 'Cape of Good Hope Factory Records'," AYB, pt. 2 (1960), 177-344.

775. _____. "John Company at the Cape," SAJE, vol. 29, no. 3 (Sept. 1961), 185-94.

776. _____. "Supplies for Napoleon's Gaolers. John Company and the Cape—St. Helena Trade during the Captivity, 1815-1821," AYB, pt. 1 (1964), 165-230.

777. Bell, C. H. "The Eighth Kaffir War," ANN, vol. 4, no. 4 (Sept. 1947), 87-97.

778. _____. "Diary of Charles Harland Bell, II," ANN, vol. 14, no. 2 (June 1960), 39-49.

779. Booyens, B. "Kerk en Staat, 1795-1843," AYB, pt. 2 (1965), 1-176.

780. Botha, C. Graham. "The Early Influence of the English Law upon the Roman-Dutch Law in South Africa," SALJ, vol. 40, pt. 4 (1923), 396-406.

781. Boucher, M. "Ex Glande Quercus. Bishop Griffith at the Cape: The Catholic Background (1803-1837) and the First Frontier 'Visitation' of 1838," Historia, vol. 11, no. 4 (Dec. 1966), 245-55.

782. Breitenbach, J. J. "The Development of the Secretaryship to the Government at the Cape of Good Hope under John Montagu, 1845-1852," AYB, pt. 2 (1959), 171-299.

783. Cory, George E. "The Rise of South Africa, Vol. VI, Chapters One to Six," AYB, pt. 1 (1939), 1-193.

784. Davies, M.A.G. "Elections in Cape Town in the Nineteenth Century," Historia, vol. 7, no. 4 (1962), 257-66.

785. DeKock, W. J. "Slaves and Slave Regulations at the Cape: 1806-1834," Historia, vol. 3, no. 3 (Sept. 1958), 202-6.

786. Duly, L. C. "The Failure of British Land Policy at the Cape, 1812-28," JAH, vol. 6, no. 3 (1965), 357-71.

787. Duminy, A. H. "The Role of Sir Andries Stockenström in Cape Politics, 1848-1856," AYB, pt. 2 (1960), 73-176.

788. Du Toit, A. E. "The Cape Frontier, a Study of Native Policy with Special Reference to the Years 1847-1866," AYB, pt. 1 (1954), vii-313.

789. Forbes, Vernon S. "The Cape Town Earthquake of December 1809," ANN, vol. 6, no. 2 (Mar. 1949), 32-36.

790. Fryer, A. K. "The Government of the Cape of Good Hope, 1825-54: The Age of Imperial Reform," AYB, pt. 1 (1964), 1-164.

791. Gailey, Harry A., Jr. "John Philip's Role in Hottentot emancipation," JAH, vol. 3, no. 3 (1962), 419-33.

792. Giliomee, H. B. "Die Administrasietydperk van Lord Caledon 1807-1811," AYB, pt. 2 (1966), 213-366.

793. Haasbroek, D.J.P. "Nie-Blanke Stemreg en Verteenwoordigende Bestuur," Historia, vol. 5, no. 2 (June 1960), 92-100.

794. Hattersley, Alan F. "Early Days of Judicial Circuits in South Africa," ANN, vol. 13, no. 4 (Dec. 1958), 122-31.

795. _____. "The Emancipation of Slaves at the Cape," History, vol. 8, no. 31 (1923), 180-86. Also in South African Quarterly, vol. 4, no. 2 (June 1922), 2-5.

796. Herrison, Charles D. "The 1837 Visit to the Cape of the French Poet Leconte de Lisle," QBSAL, vol. 13, no. 3 (Mar. 1959), 76-86.

797. Heyns, H. A. "Die Kerklike Werksaamhede van Abraham Faure," AYB, pt. 1 (1950), 29-128.

798. Holt, Basil. "Nicolaas Lochenberg. Freebooter, Elephant-hunter, and Fugitive from Justice," ANN, vol. 11, no. 1 (Dec. 1953), 3-9.

799. _____. "The War of the Axe: As Experienced by John Brownlee and Others," ANN, vol. 16, no. 8 (Dec. 1965), 328-32.

800. Hunt, Keith S. "The Development of Municipal Government in the Eastern Province of the Cape of Good Hope, with Special Reference to Grahamstown, 1827-1862," AYB (1961), 129-290.

801. Le Cordeur, B. A. "Robert Godlonton as Architect of Frontier Opinion, 1850-1857," AYB, pt. 2 (1959), vii-176.

802. Leverton, Basil J. T. "Government Finance and Political Development in the Cape, 1806-1834," AYB (1961), 291-359.

803. Lewin, Julius. "Dr. John Philip and Liberalism," Race Relations Journal, vol. 27, no. 2 (April-June 1960), 82-90.

804. Long, Una. " 'Price Control' in the Province of Queen Adelaide," ANN, vol. 6, no. 3 (June 1949), 68-72.

805. Muller, C.F.J. "Die Besoek van die Amerikaanse Oorlogsfregat 'Potomac' aan die Kaap in 1831," <u>Hertzog-Annale</u>, vol. 2 (Dec. 1955), 46-74.

806. Nobbs, Eric A. "William Duckitt's Diary," <u>AYB</u>, pt. 2 (1942), 71-90.

807. Oliver, H. G. "Exhibition to Commemorate the Centenary of Bishop Robert Gray," <u>ANN</u>, vol. 3, no. 4 (Sept. 1946), 108-12.

808. Pigott, W. H. "Historical Sketch of Farming in Albany," <u>RSAAAS</u>, vol. 5 (1908), 269-73.

809. Rennie, John V. L. "The Eastern Province as a Geographical Region," <u>SAGJ</u>, vol. 27 (1945), 1-27.

810. Reyburn, H. A. "Studies in Cape Frontier History," <u>The Critic</u>, vol. 3 (1934-35), 40-56, 101-9, 148-63, 204-9; vol. 4 (1935-36), 47-59, 105-16.

811. Roberts, Michael. "Lord Charles Somerset and the 'Beaufort Influence'," <u>AYB</u>, pt. 2 (1951), 1-34.

812. Robinson, A. M. Lewin. "Emigration to the Cape a Hundred Years Ago," <u>QBSAL</u>, vol. 2, no. 4 (June 1948), 112-16.

813. _____, ed. "The Journal of Robert Warden, Seaman, at the Cape 1796-7," <u>QBSAL</u>, vol. 7, no. 3-4 (March-June 1953), 68-79.

814. _____. "Thomas Pringle and Sir Walter Scott," <u>QBSAL</u>, vol. 6, no. 2 (Dec. 1951), 50-56; vol. 6, no. 4 (June 1952), 109-18.

815. Rochlin, S. A. "Origins of Islam in the Eastern Cape," <u>ANN</u>, vol. 12, no. 1 (Mar. 1956), 21-25.

816. Rose, J. Holland. "The French East-Indian Expedition at the Cape in 1803," <u>English Historical Review</u>, vol. 15, no. 57 (1900), 129-32.

817. Spohr, O. H. "Miscellaneous Notes on Some Libraries, Book Sales, and Early Authors in Cape Town in the Early 19th Century," <u>QBSAL</u>, vol. 19, no. 2 (Dec. 1964), 36-48.

818. Steytler, F. A. "I. 'Dag Verhaal' van Eerw. Erasmus Smit, 1815. II. 'Journal' van William F. Corner, vir die Jaar 1815. III. Minutes of the First Conference held by the African Missionaries at Graaff-Reinet in August 1814," Hertzog-Annale, vol. 3 (Dec. 1956), 67-103.

819. Trapido, Stanley. "The Origins of the Cape Franchise Qualifications of 1853," JAH, vol. 5, no. 1 (1964), 37-54.

820. Turner, L.C.F. "The Cape of Good Hope and the Anglo-French Conflict, 1797-1806," Historical Studies, Australia and New Zealand, vol. 9, no. 36 (May 1961), 368-78.

821. Tylden, G. "Major-General Sir Henry Somerset, 1794-1862," JSAHR, vol. 22 (Spring 1943), 27-34.

822. _____. "The Third Kaffir War, 1799-1802," JSAHR, vol. 37, no. 150 (June 1959), 72-82.

823. Van der Vyver, W. B. "Die Geskiedenis van die Stellenbosch Gemeente 1800-1830," AYB, pt. 1 (1958), 215-337.

824. Van der Westhuizen, W. S. "Onderwys onder die Algemene Skoolkommissie: die Periode 1804-39," AYB, pt. 2 (1953), vii-240.

825. Van Oordt, L. C. "Die Kaapse Taalargief, 5. Afrikaans-Hollandse briewe uit die jare 1798-1802, hoofsaaklik van veldkornette aan landdroste," TWK (New Series), vol. 10, no. 1 (April 1950), 65-88.

826. _____. "Die Kaapse Taalargief, 6. Afrikaans-Hollandse briewe en verklarings uit die jare 1801-1810, hoofsaaklik van veldkornette aan landdroste," TWK (New Series), vol. 11, no. 1 (April 1951), 55-75.

827. _____. "Die Kaapse Taalargief, 7. Afrikaans-Hollandse briewe uit die jare 1810-1812, hoofsaaklik van veldkornette aan landdroste," TWK (New Series), vol. 12, no. 1 (April 1952), 73-101.

828. _____. "Die Kaapse Taalargief, 8. Dertig Afrikaans-Hollandse briewe uit die jare 1812-1817, hoofsaaklik van veldkornette aan landdroste," TWK (New Series), vol. 13, no. 1 (April 1953), 45-73.

829. Van Oordt, L. C. "Die Kaapse Taalargief, 9. Sewe-en-Twintig Afrikaans-Hollandse briewe uit die jare 1817-1831, hoofsaaklik van veldkornette aan landdroste," TWK (New Series), vol. 14, no. 1 (April 1954), 33-56.

830. Varley, D. H. "The Note-Books of Arthur Barker, 1820 Settler," QBSAL, vol. 13, no. 3 (Mar. 1959), 73-76.

831. V.[arley], D. H. "Letters of Joseph Holland, 1820 Settler and Indian Corn-Grower," QBSAL, vol. 8, no. 3 (Mar.-June 1954), 92-94.

832. Wilson, N. W., tr. "A Russian View of the Cape in 1853," QBSAL, vol. 15, no. 2 (Dec. 1960), 48-76; vol. 15, no. 3 (Mar. 1961), 83-111; vol. 15, no. 4 (June 1961), 134-52; vol. 16, no. 1 (Sept. 1961), 31-48.

See also: II, VI, VIII, IX, X-B, XIII, XVII

XV   THE GREAT TREK AND ITS AFTERMATH, 1834-1854

833. Agar-Hamilton, J.A.I. "The Voortrekkers and the Natives," Race Relations, vol. 5, no. 4 (Nov. 1938), 72-76.

834. Barnard, B. J. " 'n Lewensbeskrywing van Majoor Henry Douglas Warden," AYB, pt. 1 (1948), 313-488.

835. Berthoud, Dorette. "Le Grand Trek et la Vie Boer au XIXe Siècle," Mercure de France, vol. 282, no. 953 (Mar. 1, 1938), 247-69.

836. Beyers, Coenraad. "Die Groot Trek met Betrekking tot ons Nasiegroei," AYB, pt. 1 (1941), 1-19.

837. Blok, Thos. "Die Oranje-Rivier-Soewereiniteit," TWK, vol. 2 (1923-24), 9-14, 107-13, 211-21; vol. 3 (1924-25), 60-64, 163-78.

838. Bosman, I. D. "Die Ontruiming van die Oranjerivier-Soewereiniteit 1854," HS, vol. 1, no. 1 (July 1939), 26-34.

839. Breytenbach, J. H. "Die Grondstelsel van die Voortrekkers in Natal," HS, vol. 2, no. 1-2 (July-Oct. 1940), 76-86.

840. Buys, B. R. "Die Voorgeskiedenis van die 'Ou' of Utrechtse Republiek, 1840-1856," Historia, vol. 6, no. 4 (Dec. 1961), 271-82.

841. Coetzee, P. C. "Gert Maritz versus Piet Retief: 'n Studie oor Botsende Staatsopvattings," HS, vol. 3, no. 3-4 (Oct.-Dec. 1942), 153-62.

842. Cory, George, G. Preller, and W. Blommaert. "Die Retief-Dingaan-Ooreenkoms," Stellenbosch B., vol. 2, no. 1 (May 1924), 1-95.

843. De Wet, H. C. "Waar Het Piet Uys en sy Seun Dirkie Geval?" Historia, vol. 4, no. 2 (June 1959), 75-88.

844. Dicke, B. H. "The First Voortrekkers to the Northern Transvaal and the Massacre of the van Rensburg Trek," SAJS, vol. 23 (Dec. 1926), 1006-21.

845. _____. "The Northern Transvaal Voortrekkers," AYB, pt. 1 (1941), 67-170.

846. _____. "Potgieter, Trigardt, and Pretorius Searching for the van Rensburg Trek," SAJS, vol. 23 (Dec. 1926), 1022-39.

847. Du Plessis, A. J. "Die Republiek Natalia," AYB, pt. 1 (1942), 101-238.

848. Duvenage, G.D.J. "Willem Hendrik Jacobsz se Rol in die Onafhanklikheid-en Eenheidstrewe van die Voortrekkers op die Hoëveld (1847-1852)," AYB, pt. 1 (1956), 159-264.

849. Fouché, Leo. "The Historical Setting of the Great Trek," Race Relations, vol. 5, no. 4 (Nov. 1938), 71-72.

850. Hancock, W. K. "Trek," Economic History Review, vol. 10, no. 3, series 2 (1957-58), 331-39.

851. Harrington, A. L. "Constitutional Development among the Voortrekkers, 1836-56," Historia, vol. 9, no. 2 (June 1964), 136-52.

852. Hattersley, Alan F. "The Great Trek 1835-37," History, vol. 16 (April 1931), 50-54.

853. Liebenberg, B. J. "Nederland en die Voortrekkers van Natal," CUSA, C51 (1964), 60 pp.

854. MacCrone, I. D. "The Great Trek and its Centenary Celebration in the Light of Group Psychology," Race Relations, vol. 5, no. 4 (Nov. 1938), 81-83.

855. Midgely, J. F. "The Orange River Sovereignty, 1848-1854," AYB, pt. 2 (1949), 1-594.

856. Muller, C. F. J. "Karel Landman op Trek van Melkhouteboom na Bloukransrivier, Oktober 1837-Maart 1838," CUSA, C13 (1959), 33 pp.

857. _____. "Karel Landman se Trekgeselskap," Historia, vol. 1, no. 2 (Oct. 1956), 128-41.

858. _____. "Veertig Jaar uit die Lewe van die Voortrekkerleier Karel Landman (1796-1875)," HS, vol. 4, no. 1 (Mar. 1943), 1-35.

859. _____. "Waarom die Grott Trek Geslaag Het," CUSA, B12 (1960), 24 pp.

860. Murray, A. H. "The Trek and Its Legacy," Race Relations, vol. 5, no. 4 (Nov. 1938), 76-79.

861. Ploeger, J. "Die Reisbeskrywing en Indrukke van J. Pierik. 'n Dokument wat lig werp op die gebeurtenisse en toestande in die Oranjerivieroewereiniteit omstreeks 1850," HS, vol. 1, no. 1 (July 1939), 7-15.

862. _____. "Die Reisbeskrywing van Jacobus Groenendaal: 'n Blik op die Suid-Afrikaanse samelewing deur 'n Nederlandse landverhuiser in 1850," HS, vol. 2, no. 4 (July 1941), 212-18.

863. _____. "Ulrich Gerhard Lauts (1787-1865); Die Skakel tussen Nederland en die Voortrekkers," HS, vol. 1, no. 4 (May 1940), 1-27; vol. 2, no. 1-2 (July-Oct. 1940), 1-70.

864. Pretorius, Jan G. "Die Oorsake van die Groot Trek," Historia, vol. 2, no. 3 (Dec. 1957), 239-57.

865. Punt, W. "Geographic Influences on the Great Trek and Later," SAGJ, vol. 14 (1931), 26-27.

866. _____. "Trichardt Did Not Pass Through Chuniespoort," ANN, vol. 2, no. 2 (Mar. 1945), 35-48.

867. Roodt-Coetzee, K. "Susanna Smit, skryfster van die Trek," *Hertzog-Annale*, vol. 8 (Dec. 1961), 29-44.

868. Routh, C.R.N. "The Great South African Trek," *History Today*, vol. 1, no. 5 (May 1951), 7-13.

869. Spies, F. J. du T. "G. A. Odé - Sy Byrae tot ons Kennis van die Groot Trek," *Historia*, vol. 4, no. 1 (Mar. 1959), 44-50; vol. 4, no. 2 (June 1959), 119-27; vol. 4, no. 3 (Sept. 1959), 170-78; vol. 4, no. 4 (Dec. 1959), 235-45; vol. 5, no. 1 (Mar. 1960), 19-29.

870. Thom, H. B. "Die Afkoms en Familie van Gert Maritz," *HS*, vol. 3, no. 1 (Jan. 1942), 30-41.

871. _____. "Enige Nuwe Besonderhede oor Trigardt en sy Mense," *TWK* (New Series), vol. 4, no. 1 (July 1943), 62-75.

872. Tylden, G. "Boomplaats, 29 August 1848," *JSAHR*, vol. 16 (1937), 207-14.

873. _____. "The British Army in the Orange River Colony and Vicinity 1842-54," *JSAHR*, vol. 18 (1939), 67-77.

874. _____. "Vegkop, 2 October, 1836: A Reconstruction," *ANN*, vol. 14, no. 5 (Mar. 1961), 180-82.

875. _____. "The Waggon Laager," *JSAHR*, vol. 41 (Dec. 1963), 200-205.

876. Van der Merwe, A. P. "Die Ekonomiese en Maatskaplike Ontwikkeling van Ohrigstad en Lydenburg, 1845-1857," *HS*, vol. 2, no. 4 (July 1941), 204-11.

877. _____. "Die Naturelle en die Maatskappy te Ohrigstad en Lydenburg (1845-1857)," *HS*, vol. 2, no. 1-2 (July-Oct. 1940), 87-103.

878. _____. "Die Stigting van Lydenburg," *HS*, vol. 1, no. 4 (May 1940), 28-34.

879. Van Jaarsveld, F. A. "Anthropo-Geographical Aspects of the Great Trek, 1836-1863," *Historia*, vol. 8, no. 2 (June 1963), 93-99.

880. _____. "Die Ontstaansgeskiedenis van die Begrippe 'Voortrekkers' en 'Groot Trek'," *Hertzog-Annale*, vol. 2 (Dec. 1955), 75-94.

881. Van Jaarsveld, F. A. "Die Traktaat van Zandrivier, 'n herdenking," TWK (New Series), vol. 11, no. 2 (Oct. 1951), 190-99.

882. _____. "Die tydgenootlike beoordeling van die Groot Trek," Hertzog-Annale, vol. 9 (Dec. 1962), 32-42.

883. _____. "Die tydgenootlike beoordeling van die Groot Trek, 1836-1842," CUSA, C36 (1962), 56 pp.

884. Van Schoor, M.C.E. "Die Nasionale en Politieke Bewuswording van die Afrikaner in Migrasie en sy Ontluiking in Transgariep tot 1854," AYB, pt. 2 (1963), 3-158.

885. _____. "Politieke Groeperinge in Transgariep," AYB, pt. 2 (1950), vii-186.

886. _____. "Troubreuk of Misverstand? Die Voorspel tot die Proklamering van die Oranjerivier-Soewereiniteit, 3 Feb. 1848," HS, vol. 9, no. 1-2 (Aug. 1948), 1-16.

887. Wichmann, F.A.F. "Die Nedersetting te Ohrigstad," HS, vol. 1, no. 1 (July 1939), 16-25.

888. _____. "Die Wordingsgeskiedenis van die Zuid-Afrikaansche Republiek, 1838-1860," AYB, pt. 2 (1941), 1-255.

889. Wood, W. Seals. "A Note on the Retief-Dingaan Treaty," South African Quarterly, vol. 5, no. 2 (June-Aug. 1923), 2-4.

See also: I, X-C, X-D, X-E, X-F, X-G, XIV, XVI, XVII, XIX, XX

XVI   NATAL BEFORE THE GREAT TREK

890. Geyser, O. "Die Eerste Blankes in Natal met Spesiale Verwysing na die Farewell-Tsjaka Ooreenkoms," Historia, vol. 9, no. 2 (June 1964), 129-35.

891. Hattersley, Alan F. "Francis George Farewell and the Earliest Natal Settlers," ANN, vol. 14, no. 8 (Dec. 1961), 315-20.

892. Leverton, B. "The Papers of Henry Francis Fynn," Historia, vol. 9, no. 1 (Mar. 1964), 29-33.

893. Rochlin, S. A. "Nathaniel Isaacs and Natal," Transactions of the Jewish Historical Society of England, vol. 13 (1932-35), 247-70.

See also: X-C

XVII   NATAL AFTER THE BRITISH ANNEXATION IN 1843

894. Bosch, Donald William. "The Wilgefontein Settlement, 1880," AYB, pt. 1 (1964), 231-81.

895. Conway, Alan. "Welsh Soldiers in the Zulu War," National Library of Wales Journal, vol. 11, no. 1 (Summer, 1959), 86-98.

896. Davenport, T.R.H. "The Responsible Government Issue in Natal, 1880-1882," Butterworth's South African Law Review (1957), 84-133.

897. Evans, Maurice S. "Address by the President of Section D. A Survey of the Past and Present Relations of the European and Bantu Races in Natal and Surrounding Territories," RSAAAS, vol. 13, no. 3 (Oct. 1916), 117-28.

898. Grylls, R. Glynn. "Bishop Colenso of Natal," Contemporary Review, vol. 184, no. 1051 (July 1953), 27-32.

899. Hammond, E. "The Settlement of the Byrne Immigrants in Natal, 1849-1852," SAJS, vol. 24 (Dec. 1927), 599-606.

900. Hattersley, Alan F. "The Zulu Problem of 1878-9," History, vol. 2 (April 1917), 25-32.

901. Henochsberg, Edgar S. "The Passing of the Natal Native High Court," SALJ, vol. 71, pt. 3 (Aug. 1954), 221-31.

902. Holt, Basil. "Sidney Turner and the Zulu War," QBSAL, vol. 10, no. 1 (Sept. 1955), 13-16.

903. Hutton, Edward. "Some Recollections of the Zulu war, 1879," Army Quarterly, vol. 16 (April 1928), 65-80.

904. Jackson, F.W.D. "Isandhlwana, 1879—The Sources Re-examined," JSAHR, vol. 43 (Mar. 1965), 30-43; (Sept. 1965), 113-32; (Dec. 1965), 169-83.

905. Le Cordeur, B. A. "Natal, the Cape and the Indian Ocean, 1846-1880," <u>JAH</u>, vol. 7, no. 2 (1966), 247-62.

906. Leverton, B.J.T. "The Natal Cotton Industry, 1845-75. A Study in Failure," <u>CUSA</u>, C41 (1963), 38 pp.

907. _____. "Walter Harding," <u>Historia</u>, vol. 8, no. 2 (June 1963), 104-14.

908. Marks, Shula. "Harriette Colenso and the Zulus, 1874-1913," <u>JAH</u>, vol. 4, no. 3 (1963), 403-11.

909. _____. "The Nguni, the Natalians and their History," <u>JAH</u>, vol. 8, no. 3 (1967), 529-40.

910. Park, Margaret. "The History of Early Verulam, 1850-60," <u>AYB</u>, pt. 2 (1953), 241-306.

911. Ploeger, Jan. "Besonderhede uit die Kerklike Registers van 'Nieuw-Gelderland'," <u>TWK</u> (New Series), vol. 18, no. 2 (Oct. 1958), 182-91.

912. _____. "Theodorus Christiaan Colenbrander en sy Stigting 'Nieuw-Gelderland' in Natal," <u>TWK</u> (New Series), vol. 18, no. 1 (April 1958), 43-60.

913. Robertson, H. M. "The 1849 Settlers in Natal," <u>SAJE</u>, vol. 17, no. 3 (Sept. 1949), 274-88; vol. 17, no. 4 (Dec. 1949), 416-42.

914. Savage, M. B., ed. "Intombi River Drift, March 1879: A Contemporary Letter written by Major Charles Tucker," <u>JSAHR</u>, vol. 22 (Spring 1944), 180-86.

915. Trapido, Stanley. "Natal's Non-Racial Franchise, 1856," <u>AS</u>, vol. 22, no. 1 (1963), 22-32.

916. Tucker, W. P. "The Progress of the Natal Sugar Industry from Its Inception in 1851 up to 1915," <u>RSAAAS</u>, vol. 13, no. 10 (June 1917), 516-20.

917. Turner, Lorenzo D. "The Odyssey of a Zulu Warrior," <u>Journal of Negro History</u>, vol. 40, no. 4 (Oct. 1955), 305-17.

918. Tylden, G. "Some Aspects of the Zulu Wars," <u>JSAHR</u>, vol. 17 (1938), 127-32.

919. Tylden, G. "The British Army in Zululand, 1883 to 1888," JSAHR, vol. 29 (1951), 48-51.

920. _____. "Inhlobane Mountain and Kambula, Zululand, 28th-29th March, 1879," JSAHR, vol. 31 (1953), 3-9.

921. _____. "The 27th Inniskilling Regiment in Natal, 1841-45," JSAHR, vol. 29 (1951), 106-11.

922. Van Zyl, M. C. "Die Koms van die Boere na Zoeloeland in 1884. Genooides of Indringers?" CUSA, C37 (1962).

923. _____. "Luitenant-goewerneur Martin West en die Natalse Voortrekkers, 1845-1849," AYB, pt. 2 (1955), 113-86.

924. _____. "Die Uitbreiding van Britse Gesag oor die Natalse Noordgrensgebiede (1879-1897)," AYB, pt. 1 (1966), 1-299.

925. Wheeler-Holohan, V. "Fifty Years Ago: Isandhlwana, the 22nd of January, 1879," Army Quarterly, vol. 18, no. 2 (July 1929), 316-24.

926. Whitton, F. E. "Isandhlwana: January 22, 1879," The Twentieth Century, vol. 105 (Jan. 1929), 114-26.

927. Young, Lindsay M. "The Native Policy of Benjamin Pine in Natal, 1850-55," AYB, pt. 2 (1951), 209-346.

See also: VI, X-C, XV, XVIII, XXIV

XVIII   THE CAPE COLONY, 1854-1899

928. Brownlee, Frank. "The Administration of the Transkeian Native Territories," JRAS, vol. 36 (July 1937), 337-46.

929. Campbell, W. B. "The South African Frontier, 1865-1885. A Study in Expansion," AYB, pt. 2 (1959), 1-242.

930. De Kock, W. J. "Ekstraterritoriale Vraagstukke van die Kaapse Regering (1872-1885) met besondere verwysing na die Transgariep en Betsjoeanaland," AYB, pt. 1 (1948), 1-306.

931. Holt, Basil. "The Battle of Maxongo's Hoek," ANN, vol. 11, no. 8 (Sept. 1955), 310-16.

932. Holt, Basil. "Old Forts of the Transkei," ANN, vol. 11, no. 6 (Mar. 1955), 197-202.

933. Kirby, Percival R. "Fort Brown (Hermanus Kraal)," ANN, vol. 12, no. 1 (Mar. 1956), 5-10.

934. Le Cordeur, B. A. "The Relations between the Cape and Natal (1846-1879)," AYB (1965), 1-264.

935. Lewsen, Phyllis. "The First Crisis in Responsible Government in the Cape Colony," AYB, pt. 2 (1942), 205-66.

936. Lombard, P. J. "Die Stigting en Vroeë Geskiedenis van Queenstown, 1853-1859," AYB, pt. 2 (1952), 77-192.

937. P.C.G. "Colonial Law and Native Custom," SALJ, vol. 28, pt. 1 (1911), 68-72; vol. 28, pt. 3, 341-48.

938. Trapido, Stanley. "African divisional politics in the Cape Colony, 1884 to 1910," JAH, vol. 9, no. 1 (1968), 79-98.

939. Tylden, G. "The Capture of Morosi's Mountain, 1879," JSAHR, vol. 15 (1936), 208-15.

940. _____. "The Frontier Light Horse, 1877-79," JSAHR, vol. 18 (1939), 224-27.

941. _____. "A Note on the 'Edwards Papers', Basutoland, June to September 1881," ANN, vol. 9, no. 4 (Sept. 1952), 133-34.

942. _____. "The Permanent Colonial Forces of Cape Colony," JSAHR, vol. 19 (1940), 149-59.

943. _____. "The Senior South African Regular Regiment, 1852 to 1950," ANN, vol. 8, no. 1 (Dec. 1950), 2-33.

944. _____. "South Africa, 1877-78, the Ninth Kaffir War," JSAHR, vol. 20 (1941), 226-32.

945. Venter, P. J. "An Early Botanist and Conservationist at the Cape, The Reverend John Croumbie Brown, LL.D, F.R.G.S., F.L.S.," AYB, pt. 2 (1952), 279-93.

See also: IX, X-B, X-D, XIII, XIV, XV, XIX, XXI, XXV

946.   Attree, E. M. "The Closer Union Movements between the Orange Free State, South African Republic and Cape Colony (1838-1863)," AYB, pt. 1 (1949), 303-77.

947.   Fourie, P. C. "Die Administrasie van die Oranje-Vrystaat tot 1859," AYB, pt. 2 (1963), 159-246.

948.   _____. "President Boshof en die Staatsdiens van die Oranje-Vrystaat," Historia, vol. 5, no. 4 (Dec. 1960), 273-80.

949.   Francken, A. "Uit het Lewen van Dr. Brill," TWK, vol. 3 (1924-25), 198-203; vol. 4, no. 1 (Aug. 1925), 31-37; vol. 4, no. 2 (Nov. 1925), 78-83.

950.   Grimsehl, H. W. "Die Rol van Stephanus Schoeman tydens die Burgeroorlog (1861-1864)," Historia, vol. 2, no. 3 (Dec. 1957), 227-38.

951.   Grobbelaar, J.J.G. "Die Vrystaatse Republiek en die Basoetoe-vraagstuk," AYB, pt. 2 (1939), 1-205.

952.   Jacobs, David Stephanus. "Abraham Fischer in sy Tydperk (1850-1913)," AYB, pt. 2 (1965), 177-437.

953.   Kriel, J. D. "Die Verhouding tussen Kerk en Staat in die Republiek van die Oranje-Vrystaat (1854-1902)," AYB, pt. 1 (1953), 155-268.

954.   Malan, J. H. "Uit die Bloemfonteinse Argief. John X. Merriman aan President Brand," TWK, vol. 1 (1922-23), 169-79.

955.   Meyer, S. "Kommandant Louw Wepener," Historia, vol. 7, no. 3 (1962), 164-79.

956.   Ploeger, Jan. "Besonderhede in verband met die geslag Boshoff; met besondere verwysing na wyle Stattspresident Jacobus Nicolaas Boshof(f)," HS, vol. 4, no. 1 (Mar. 1943), 36-59.

957.   Sandler, E. M. "Adolph Coqui - Geleerde Swerwer," Historia, vol. 11, no. 2 (June 1966), 112-19.

958.   Thompson, Leonard M. "Constitutionalism in the South African Republics," Butterworth's South African Law Review (1954), 49-72.

959. Van der Merwe, J. "Die Kliprivier-Grenskwessie tussen die Suid-Afrikaanse Republiek en die Oranje-Vrystaat," <u>HS</u>, vol. 1 (July 1939), 35-43.

960. Van Jaarsveld, F. A. "Die Vrystaat-Transvaalse Vriendskaps-verdrag van 1872," <u>Historia</u>, vol. 2, no. 2 (Sept. 1957), 148-62.

961. Van Rensburg, A.P.J. "Die Rol deur Landdroste, Vrederegters en Veldkornette in die distrik Bloemfontein vanaf 1854-1880 gespeel," <u>AYB</u>, pt. 2 (1954), 185-308.

962. Venter, I.S.J. "Die Anglikaanse Kerk en sy Stryd om Staatsondersteuning in die Oranje-Vrystaatse Republiek," <u>CUSA</u>, C4 (1958), 64 pp.

963. Venter, W. A. "Die Geskiedenis van die Nederduitse Gereformeerde Gemeente Bloemfontein gedurende die Pioniersjare (1848-1880)," <u>AYB</u> (1962), 163-306.

See also: VI, X-D, XV, XX, XXI

XX   THE TRANSVAAL, 1852-1899

964. Anon. "The Years before the Raid," <u>Quarterly Review</u>, vol. 191, no. 381 (1900), 222-45.

965. Backeberg, H.E.W. "Die Betrekkinge tussen die Suid-Afrikaanse Republiek en Duitsland tot na die Jameson-Inval (1852-1896)," <u>AYB</u>, pt. 1 (1949), 1-302.

966. _____. "Die Politieke Betekenis von die Eerste Hermanns-burgse Sendelinge op die Transvaalse Wesgrens. Die Pad na die Noorde (1857-64)," <u>HS</u>, vol. 1, no. 2 (Oct. 1939), 12-21.

967. Basson, M.A. "Die Britse Invloed in die Transvaalse Onderwys 1836-1907," <u>AYB</u>, pt. 2 (1956), 1-282.

968. Beyers, Coenraàd. "Die Wapen van die Suid-Afrikaanse Republiek," <u>AYB</u>, pt. 1, (1950), 1-28.

969. Bond, Brian. "The Disaster at Majuba Hill, 1881," <u>History Today</u>, vol. 15 (1965), 486-95.

970. Breytenbach, J. H. "Andries François du Toit; Sy Aandeel in die Transvaalse Geskiedenis," AYB, pt. 2 (1942), 1-70.

971. Buys, M. H. "Die Ontwikkeling van die Kantoor van die Staatsekretaris van die Z.A.R.," Historia, vol. 7, no. 1 (Mar. 1962), 39-46.

972. Cloete, J.J.N. "Munisipale Stemreg in die Zuid-Afrikaansche Republiek," Historia, vol. 3, no. 2 (June 1958), 89-96.

973. _____. "Die Ontstaan en Ontwikkeling van die Munisipale Bestuur en Administrasie van Pretoria tot 1910," AYB, pt. 1 (1960), 1-267.

974. De Vaal, J. B. "Opvoeding in Schoemansdal 1848-1867," HS, vol. 1, no. 2 (Oct. 1939), 25-30.

975. _____. "Die Rol van João Albasini in die Geskiedenis van die Transvaal," AYB, pt. 1 (1953), vii-154.

976. Du Plessis, J. S. "Die Ontstaan en Ontwikkeling van die Staatspresident in die Zuid-Afrikaansche Republiek (1858-1902," AYB, pt. 1 (1955), xi -283.

977. Du Plessis, T. A. "Jacobus Stuart en die Transvaalse Verdeeldheid van 1855-56," HS, vol. 8, no. 1 (June 1947), 33-39.

978. Forsyth, D. R. "Johannesburg Vrijwilliger Corps, 1894-1899. Commandant S. H. van Diggelen," ANN, vol. 13, no. 7 (Sept. 1959), 246-71; vol. 14, no. 6 (June 1961), 208-28.

979. Fouché, L. "Johannesburg in South African History," SAJS, vol. 33 (Mar. 1937), 1127-36.

980. Grey, P. C. "Eilande in die Vaalrivier. Die oplossing van 'n grenskwessie tussen die Suid-Afrikaanse Republiek en die Oranje-Vrystaat 1884-1895," CUSA, C56 (1965), 62 pp.

981. Grimsehl, H. W. "Onluste in Modjadjiland, 1890-1894," AYB, pt. 2 (1955), 187-254.

982. Haasbroek, D.J.P. "Potchefstroom se Status en Verhouding tot die Res van die Voortrekkergemeenskap," Historia, vol. 1, no. 3 (Feb. 1957), 239-54.

983. Haupt, D. J. "Die Staatsartillerie van die Suid-Afrikaanse Republiek," HS, vol. 8, no. 3-4 (April 1948), 175-90.

984. Henry, James A. "The Standard Bank's Early Days in Johannesburg, 1886-1900," ANN, vol. 12, no. 3 (Sept. 1956), 83-94.

985. Heijstek, J. L. K. "Vroegste Wetgewing in Transvaal i.v.m. Immigrasie," HS, vol. 1, no. 2 (Oct. 1939), 5-11.

986. Hugo, Maria. "Die Kruger-Ultimatum (Vier Maande van Spanning)," HS, vol. 4, no. 3-4 (Oct.-Dec. 1943), 117-208.

987. _____. "Die stemregvraagstuk in die Zuid-Afrikaansche Republiek," AYB (1947), 1-196.

988. Kahn, Ellison. "The History of the Administration of Justice in the South African Republic," SALJ, vol. 75, pt. 3 (Aug. 1958), 294-317; vol. 75, pt. 4 (Nov. 1958), 397-417; vol. 76, pt. 1 (Feb. 1959), 46-57.

989. Kistner, W. "The Anti-Slavery Agitation against the Transvaal Republic, 1852-1868," AYB, pt. 2 (1952), 193-278.

990. Krüger, B. J. "Bantoe-Arbeid in die Suid-Afrikaanse Republiek soos Benader deur die Boere en die Sendelinge," Historia, vol. 11, no. 2 (June 1966), 82-95.

991. _____. "Diskussies en wetgewing rondom die landelike arbeidsvraagstuk in die Suid-Afrikaanse Republiek met besondere verwysing na die Plakkerswelte, 1885-1899," CUSA, C62 (1966), 66 pp.

992. _____. "Hoe die Transvaalse Boer die Bantoe Gesien Het," Historia, vol. 10, no. 3 (Sept. 1965), 176-85.

993. Krüger, D. W. "Die Weg na die See," AYB, pt. 1 (1938), 31-233.

994. Kuit, Albert. "Generaal Joubert besoek Europa en Amerika," HS, vol. 6, no. 2 (June 1945), 45-67.

995. Lohman, W. H. de Savornin. "De oudste beschrijving van de Transvaal en haar auteur Jacobus Stuart (9 Febr. 1803-15 Sept. 1878)," Bijdragen voor Vaderlandsche Geschiedenis en Oudheidkunde, series 4, vol. 10, no. 3 (1911), 260-79.

996. Lombaard, B. V. "Die Herinneringe van Kommandant J. Carel Winterbach (1850-1907)," HS, vol. 5, no. 3 (Sept. 1944), 127-52.

997. Mawby, A. A. "The Right Rev. Dr. Henry Brougham Bousfield, First (Anglican) Bishop of Pretoria: The First Phase in the Transvaal (1879-1886)," Historia, vol. 8, no. 2 (June 1963), 81-87.

998. Mouton, J.A. "Generaal Piet Joubert en sy aandeel aan die Transvaalse Geskiedenis," AYB, pt. 1 (1957), 1-292.

999. Nell, P. R. "Die Konsulêre en Diplomatieke Verteenwoordiging van die Suid-Afrikaanse Republiek in die Buiteland," HS, vol. 6, no. 3 (Sept. 1945), 93-193.

1000. Otto, J. C. "Die Regsgronde vir die Grondbesit deur Boere in Noord-Oostlike Transvaal," HS, vol. 1, no. 4 (May 1940), 46-59.

1001. Pelzer, A. N. "Die Eerste Diplomatieke Verteenwoordiging van die Suid-Afrikaanse Republiek in Engeland," Historia, vol. 1, no. 1 (June 1956), 37-48.

1002. _____. "Die 'Arm-Blanke' in die Suid-Afrikaanse Republiek tussen die Jare 1882 en 1899," HS, vol. 2, no. 3 (Jan. 1941), 123-50; vol. 2, no. 4 (July 1941), 179-203.

1003. _____. "Die Ingebruikstelling van Papiergeld in die Suid-Afrikaanse Republiek," Historia, vol. 10, no. 4 (Dec. 1965), 228-45; vol. 11, no. 1 (Mar. 1966), 4-17.

1004. Pieterse, D. J. "Die Geskiedenis van die Mynindustrie in Transvaal, 1836-1886," AYB (1943), 73-212.

1005. Ploeger, Jan. "Die Afbakening van die Grens tussen die Z.A.R. en Mosambiek by Komatiepoort (1887)," HS, vol. 3, no. 2 (May 1942), 87-89.

1006. _____. "Dr. Eduard Johan Pieter Jorissen (10 Junie 1829-20 Maart 1912)," TWK (New Series), vol. 6, no. 1 (Nov. 1945), 39-78.

1007. _____. "Nuwe Gegewens Aangaande Hendrik Stiemens (1822-1894)," Historia, vol. 4, no. 2 (June 1959), 89-112.

1008. Ploeger, Jan. "Onderwys en Onderwys Joeleid in die Suid-Afrikaanse Republiek onder Ds. S. J. du Toit en Dr. N. Mansvelt (1881-1900)," AYB, pt. 1 (1952), 1-267.

1009. _____. "Die Reisbeskrywing van Dr. E.J.P. Jorissen," Hertzog-Annale, vol. 5 (Dec. 1958), 112-34.

1010. _____. "Uit die Briewe van Antony de Vletter...Eerste Onderwyser en Posmeester van Dullstroom (1882-1888)," Historia, vol. 7, no. 2 (June 1962), 106-20.

1011 _____. "Die Zuid-Afrikaansche Republiek deur Nederland Erken as 'n Selfstandige Staat," HS, vol. 1, no. 3 (Jan. 1940), 28-32.

1012. Potgieter, F. J. "Die Vestiging van die Blanke in Transvaal (1837-86) met spesiale verwysing na die verhouding tussen die mens en die omgewing," AYB, pt. 2 (1958), vii-208.

1013. Pretorius, H. S. "Afkoms van Paul Kruger," HS, vol. 4, no. 3-4 (Oct.-Dec. 1943), 209-22.

1014. Reyneke, C.J.J. "Landdros en Heemrade se Rol in die Plaaslike Bestuur van die Republiek Lydenburg," HS, vol. 8, no. 3-4 (April 1948), 192-97.

1015. _____. "Landdros en Heemrade se Rol in die Regspraak van die Republiek Lydenburg," HS, vol. 9, no. 1-2 (Aug. 1948), 28-34.

1016. Reyneke, G. J. "Utrecht in die Geskiedenis van die Transvaal tot 1877," AYB, pt. 2 (1958), 209-81.

1017. Rochlin, S. A. "Early Impressions of the Witwatersrand," ANN, vol. 12, no. 3 (Sept. 1956), 104-9.

1018. Schapera, Isaac. "Livingstone and the Boers," African Affairs, vol. 59, no. 235 (1960), 144-56.

1019. Tomlinson, F. R., D.J.G Smith, and H.A. Kotze. "Honderd Jaar Landbou in die Transvaal," TWK (New Series), vol. 16, no. 2 (Oct. 1956), 144-56.

1020. 'Transvaal Lawyer'. "The Franchise Laws of the Transvaal," Cape Law Journal, vol. 12 (1895), 87-95.

1021. Tylden, G. "Majuba, 27th February, 1881. A Contemporary Boer Account," JSAHR, vol. 17 (1938), 9-12.

1022. _____. "A Study in Attack: Majuba, 27th February, 1881," JSAHR, vol. 39 (Mar. 1961), 27-36.

1023. Van Coller, H. P. "Veldkornet Stephanus Johannes Roos," HS, vol. 2, no. 3 (Jan. 1941), 151-61.

1024. Van den Bergh, C. N. "The Police System in the South African Republic before 1881," Historia, vol. 2, no. 1 (June 1957), 67-73.

1025. Van Heerden, Jacobus Johannes. "Die Kommandant-Generaal in die Geskiedenis van die Suid-Afrikaanse Republiek," AYB, pt. 2 (1964), 1-198.

1026. _____. "Die Kommandant-Generaal in die Suid-Afrikaanse Republiek tot 1860," HS, vol. 5, no. 4 (Dec. 1944), 187-265.

1027. Van Jaarsveld, F. A. "Landmeting in die Ou Dae," HS, vol. 8, no. 1 (June 1947), 45-53.

1028. _____. "Transvaal en die Tweede Basoeto-Oorlog," Historia, vol. 1, no. 1 (June 1956), 52-61; vol. 1, no. 2 (Oct. 1956), 167-76.

1029. _____. "Die Transvaalse Presidents Verkiesing van 1871-1872," TWK (New Series), vol. 17, no. 1 (April 1957), 21-46.

1030. _____. "Veldkornet A. P. van der Walt, die man op wie se plaas Pretoria uitgelê is," TWK (New Series), vol. 15, no. 2 (Oct. 1955), 104-44.

1031. _____. "Die Veldkornet en sy aandeel in die opbou van die Suid-Afrikaanse Republiek tot 1870," AYB, pt. 2 (1950), 187-354.

1032. Van Rooyen, T. S. "Die Sendeling Alexander Merensky in die Geskiedenis van die Suid-Afrikaanse Republiek, 1859-1882," AYB, pt. 2 (1954), 97-184.

1033. _____. "Die Verhoudinge tussen die Boere, Engelse en Naturelle in die Geskiedenis van die Oos-Transvaal tot 1882," AYB (1951), 1-376.

1034. Van Winter, P. J. "De Nederlandsche Zuid-Afrikaansche Spoorweg-Maatschappij, de Zuid-Afrikaansche Republiek en de Unie van Zuid-Afrika," <u>HS</u>, vol. 8, no. 3-4 (April 1948), 119-37.

1035. Verburgh, C. "The Competition of South African Harbours and Lourenço Marques for the Oceanborne Imports of the Transvaal 'Competitive Area'," <u>SAJE</u>, vol. 25, no. 4 (Dec. 1957), 264-74.

1036. Weidemann, N. C. "Die Malaboch-Oorlog (1894)," <u>HS</u>, vol. 7, no. 1 (Mar. 1946), 1-48.

1037. Wypkema, A. "Die Volkstemidee in Suid-Afrika," <u>HS</u>, vol. 1, no. 1 (July 1939), 48-59.

<u>See also</u>: I, II, X-E, X-G, XV, XIX, XXIV, XXV

XXI   LESOTHO, BOTSWANA, AND SWAZILAND

1038. Agar-Hamilton, J.A.I. "The South African Protectorates," <u>JAS</u>, vol. 29 (1929-30), 12-26.

1039. Coryndon, R. T. "Swaziland," <u>JAS</u>, vol. 14 (April 1915), 250-65.

1040. Dumas, Charles E. F. "A Huguenot Missionary, or, The Late Eugène Casalis," <u>Proceedings of the Huguenot Society of London</u>, vol. 19, no. 4 (1956), 106-12.

1041. Garson, Noel George. "The Swaziland Question and a Road to the Sea (1887-1895)," <u>AYB</u>, pt. 2 (1957), 263-438.

1042. Tylden, G. "The Affair at the Berea Mountain, 20th December, 1852," <u>JSAHR</u>, vol. 14, no. 53 (Spring 1935), 33-45.

1043. _____. "The Bechuanaland Border Police, 1885-1895," <u>JSAHR</u>, vol. 19 (1940), 236-42.

1044. Van der Poel, Jean. "Basutoland as a Factor in South African Politics (1858-1870)," <u>AYB</u>, pt. 1 (1941), 171-230.

1045. Venter, I.S.J. "Die Rol van die Drukpers in die Wesleyaanse Betsjoeanasending Gedurende die Halfeeu 1825-1875," <u>Historia</u>, vol. 4, no. 3 (Sept. 1959), 161-69.

1046. Venter, I.S.J. "Die Ruilkontrakte in 1833-34 aangegaan tussen Mosjesj en die Wesleyane," CUSA, C20 (1960), 55 pp.

1047. _____. "Die Sendingstasie Thaba Nchu 1833-1900," CUSA, C18 (1960), 56 pp.

1048. Venter, W. A. "Die Familietwis in die Swazi-Koningshuis: Was Buitestaanders Aandadig?," Historia, vol. 10, no. 2 (June 1965), 130-33.

See also: X-C, X-D, X-F, XIX, XX, XXV

XXII   SOUTH-WEST AFRICA

1049. Bruwer, J. P. van S. "Suidwes-Afrika sedert Maharero," JSWASS, vol. 16 (1961-1962), 73-79.

1050. Lehmann, Rudolf F. "Die Verhouding van die Duitse Beskermingsadministrasie in Suidwes Afrika tot die Ambovolke," JSWASS, vol. 11 (1955-1956), 5-32.

1051. Norton, W. A. "The South-West Protectorate and its Native Population," RSAAAS, vol. 16, no. 5 (1920), 453-65.

1052. Rust, F. "Missionar Johann Georg Krönlein," JSWASS, vol. 18-19 (1963/64-1964/65), 65-72.

1053. Stals, E. L. P. "Die Geskiedenis van die Beesteelt in Suidwes-Afrika tydens die Duitse Tydperk (1884-1915)," AYB (1962), 75-162.

1054. Trümpelmann, G.P.J. "Die Boer in Suidwes-Afrika," AYB, pt. 2 (1948), 1-166.

1055. Vedder, H. "Bedeutung der Stammes-und Ortsnamen in Südwestafrika (Auf historischer Grundlage)," JSWASS, vol. 4 (1928-29), 11-28.

See also: VII, VIII, IX, X-I, XXVI

1056. Anon. "Recollections of the Rebellion, 1896," NADA, vol. 14
       (1936-37), 49-61.

1057. Barnard, M. W. "The Battle of Imbembesi," Rhodesiana,
       Publication No. 15 (Dec. 1966), 1-11.

1058. Berghegge, Francis. "Account of a Journey in Central Africa,"
       Rhodesiana, Publication No. 3 (1958), 1-13.

1059. Bolze, Louis W. "The Railway comes to Bulawayo," Rhodesiana,
       Publication No. 18 (July 1968), 47-84.

1060. Boni, Nazi. "La colonisation rhodésienne en Afrique du Sud,"
       Afrique-Documents (Dakar), nos. 76-77 (1964), 277-89.

1061. Brown, Richard. "Aspects of the Scramble for Matabeleland,"
       in Stokes, E., and R. Brown, eds., The Zambesian Past
       (Manchester, 1966), 63-93.

1062. Cripps, L. "The Umtase Treaty," NADA, vol. 11 (1933),
       91-95.

1063. Doyle, D. " 'The Rise and Fall of the Matabele Nation' 1893,"
       Rhodesiana, Publication No. 14 (July 1966), 51-60.

1064. Edwards, J. A. "The Lomagundi District: An Historical
       Sketch," Rhodesiana, Publication No. 7 (1962), 1-21.

1065. Edwards, William. " 'Wiri'. Reminiscences," NADA, vol. 37
       (1960), 81-101; vol. 38 (1961), 5-21; vol. 39 (1962), 19-44.

1066. Garlake, P. S. "Pioneer Forts in Rhodesia," Rhodesiana,
       Publication No. 12 (Sept. 1965), 37-62.

1067. Glass, S. "The Outbreak of the Matabele War (1893) in the
       Light of Recent Research," Rhodesiana, Publication No. 14
       (July 1966), 34-43.

1068. Glover, L. S. "Memories of the Mashonaland Mounted Police,
       1896-97," Rhodesiana, Publication No. 11 (Dec. 1964), 37-49.

1069. Hickman, A. S. "The Seige of the Abercorn Store," Rhodesiana,
       Publication No. 9 (Dec. 1963), 18-27.

1070. Hole, H. Marshall. "Pioneer Days in Southern Rhodesia,"
      JRAS, vol. 35 (1936), 37-47.

1071. Hoste, H. F. "Rhodesia in 1890," Rhodesiana, Publication
      No. 12 (Sept. 1965), 1-26.

1072. Howland, R. C. "The Mazoe Patrol," Rhodesiana, Publication
      No. 8 (1963), 16-33.

1073. Lloyd, M., tr. "Diaries of the Jesuit Missionaries at Bulawayo,
      1879-1881," Rhodesiana, Publication No. 4 (1959), 7-84.

1074. Maffat, R. L. "A Further Note on the Battle of Shangani,"
      Rhodesiana, Publication No. 18 (July 1968), 95-100.

1075. O'Mahoney, B.M.E. and K. E. "The Southern Column's Fight
      at Singuesi, 2nd November 1893," Rhodesiana, Publication No.
      9 (Dec. 1963), 28-36. See also Publication No. 18 (July 1968), 107-9.

1076. Pollett, Hugh. "The Mazoe Patrol," Rhodesiana, Publication
      No. 2 (1957), 29-38.

1077. Ranger, Terence. "The Role of Ndebele and Shona Religious
      Authorities in the Rebellions of 1896 and 1897," in Stokes, E.,
      and R. Brown, eds. The Zambesian Past (Manchester, 1966),
      94-136.

1078. Ransford, O. N. " 'White Man's Camp', Bulawayo," Rhodesiana,
      Publication No. 18 (July 1968), 13-21.

1079. Rea, W. F. "Rhodesian Pioneer," Rhodesiana, Publication
      No. 5 (1960), 54-59.

1080. Tabler, Edward C. "Guy Dawnay's Routes to Matabeleland and
      the Victoria Falls, 1873," ANN, vol. 13, no. 3 (Sept. 1958),
      87-93.

1081. _____. "The Tati Gold Rush and the Diary of Alexander
      Hamp," ANN, vol. 13, no. 2 (June 1958), 53-69.

1082. Walker, Eric A. "The Northern Goldfields Diaries of Thomas
      Baines, 1869-1872," International Review of Missions, vol. 36,
      no. 144 (Oct. 1947), 526-34.

1083. Warhurst, P. R., ed. "Extracts from the South African Letters and Diaries of Victor Morier, 1890-1891," Rhodesiana,
Publication no. 13 (Dec. 1965), 1-37.

See also: IV-F, VI, X-F, X-G, XXV

XXIV   THE INDIANS

1084. Anon. "The British-Asiatic Question," Cape Law Journal,
vol. 16 (1899), 102-7.

1085. Burrows, H. R. "Indian Life and Labour in Natal," Race Relations, vol. 10, no. 1 (1943), 1-36.

1086. De Kock, N. M. "Indiërs in die Suid-Afrikaanse Republiek,"
Historia, vol. 0, no. 1 (Mar. 1964), 8-28.

1087. Fannin, D. G. "The Legal Position," Race Relations, vol. 14,
no. 3 (1947), 107-19.

1088. Fouche, J. H. "Die Asiate-Vraagstuk in die Dae van die Suid-
Afrikaanse Republiek," HS, vol. 7, nos. 2-3 (June-Sept. 1946),
49-122.

1089. Huttenback, Robert A. "Indians in South Africa, 1860-1914:
The British Imperial Philosophy on Trial," English Historical
Review, vol. 81, no. 319 (April 1966), 273-91.

1090. Naidoo, V. Sirkari. "Historical Background," Race Relations,
vol. 14, no. 3 (1947), 80-88.

1091. Pachai, Bridglal. "South African Indians and Citizenship: A
Historical Survey—1855-1934," Africa Quarterly (New Delhi),
vol. 4, no. 3 (Oct.-Dec. 1964), 167-78.

1092. Thompson, Leonard M. "Indian Immigration into Natal, 1860-
1872," AYB, pt. 2 (1952), vii-76.

See also: XVII, XX

1093. Anon. "Federation in South Africa," Quarterly Review, vol. 192, no. 384 (1900), 505-19.

1094. Barnard, S. P. "Korrespondensie oor Voorgestelde Konfederasie van Suid-Afrikaanse Kolonies en State, 1876-," TWK, vol. 1 (1922-23), 42-54.

1095. Beyers, C. J. "Graham Bower en die Jameson-Inval ('n Kritiese Benadering)," HS, vol. 7, no. 4 (Dec. 1946), 133-47.

1096. Blainey, G. "Lost Causes of the Jameson Raid," Economic History Review, Second Series, vol. 18, no. 2, 350-66.

1097. Bradlow, Edna. "A South African Year of Crisis, 1899," History Today, vol. 11 (Oct. 1961), 712-19.

1098. Butler, Jeffrey. "Sir Alfred Milner on British Policy in South Africa in 1897," Boston University Papers in African History, vol. 1 (1964), 243-70.

1099. Buxton, Earl. "The Jameson Raid," JAS, vol. 30 (April 1931), 113-18.

1100. Davey, Arthur M. "The Siege of Pretoria, 1880-81," AYB, pt. 1 (1956), 265-316.

1101. Davies, Joan. "Palgrave and Damaraland," AYB, pt. 2 (1942), 91-204.

1102. De Kiewiet, C. W. "The Policy of the British Government towards the South African Dutch Republics, 1848-1872," Bulletin of the Institute of Historical Research, vol. 6, no. 16 (June 1928), 41-44.

1103. De Kock, W. J. "Die Rol van J. A. Froude in Suid-Afrika," HS, vol. 1, no. 3 (Jan. 1940), 37-46; vol. 1, no. 4 (May 1940), 35-45.

1104. Drus, Ethel. "The Question of Imperial Complicity in the Jameson Raid," English Historical Review, vol. 68, no. 269 (Oct. 1953), 582-93.

1105. _____. "A Report on the Papers of Joseph Chamberlain Relating to the Jameson Raid and the Inquiry," Bulletin of the Institute of Historical Research, vol. 25, no. 71 (1952), 33-62.

1106. Drus, Ethel. "Select documents from the Chamberlain Papers Concerning Anglo-Transvaal Relations, 1896-1899," Bulletin of the Institute of Historical Research, vol. 27, no. 76 (1954), 156-89.

1107. Fripp. C. E. "Bechuanaland and 'The North' (1880-1890)," PTRSA, vol. 42 (Mar. 1949), 96-114.

1108. Geyser, O. "Theophilus Shepstone en die Anneksasie van die Suid-Afrikaanse Republiek - 'n Nabetragting," Historia, vol. 10, no. 3 (Sept. 1965), 157-67.

1109. Hammond, John Hays. "The Jameson Raid and the World War, the True Story of the Raid," Scribner's Magazine, vol. 79, no. 3 (Mar. 1926), 227-39; vol. 79, no. 4 (Apr. 1926), 376-86.

1110. Harlow, Vincent. "Sir Frederic Hamilton's Narrative of Events relative to the Jameson Raid," English Historical Review, vol. 72, no. 283 (April 1957), 279-305.

1111. Hattersley, Alan F. "The Annexation of the Transvaal, 1877," History, vol. 21, no. 81 (June 1936), 41-47.

1112. _____. "Migration Between Canada and South Africa in Early Victorian Times," ANN, vol. 12, no. 5 (Mar. 1957), 155-61.

1113. Ireland, Alleyne. "The True Story of the Jameson Raid as Related to Me by John Hays Hammond," North American Review, vol. 208, no. 753 (Aug. 1918), 185-96; vol. 208, no. 754 (Sept. 1918), 365-76.

1114. Jenkins, P. L. "How Rhodesia Became British," PRSA, vol. 12 (1912), 45-59.

1115. Jollie, E. Tawse. "The Race for Manica," United Empire (New Series), vol. 23, no. 8 (Aug. 1932), 442-45.

1116. Kies, G.J.A. "Die Pretoria-konvensie en die Konvensie van London," Historia, vol. 4, no. 2 (June 1959), 129-36.

1117. Lombaard, S. G. "Op Amajuba," Historia, vol. 8, no. 1 (Mar. 1963), 54-59.

1118. Martineau, J. "The Transvaal Trouble; How It Arose," Quarterly Review, vol. 184, no. 368 (1896), 532-63; vol. 186. no. 371 (1897), 241-67.

1119. Oudard, G. "[Account of Cecil Rhodes]," Revue Parisienne, vol. 46, pt. 3 (May 1-June 1, 1939), 117-45, 377-409, 590-625.

1120. Pieterse, D. J. "Die Kommandeer-Vraagstuk," HS, vol. 6, no. 1 (March 1945), 1-31.

1121. _____. "Transvaal en Britse Susereiniteit, 1881-1884," AYB, pt. 1 (1940), 257-344.

1122. Ranger, Terence. "The Last Word on Rhodes?" Past and Present, no. 28 (July 1964), 116-27.

1123. Stokes, Eric. "Great Britain and Africa: The Myth of Imperialism," History Today, vol. 10 (Aug. 1960), 554-63.

1124. _____. "Milnerism," Historical Journal, vol. 5, no. 1 (1962), 47-60.

1125. Tylden, G. "The British Army and the Transvaal, 1875-1885," JSAHR, vol. 30 (1952), 159-71.

1126. Van der Walt, Hendrik Roelof. "Die Suid-Afrikaanse Republiek in die Britse Buitelandse en Koloniale Beleid (1881-1899)," AYB, pt. 1 (1963), 1-295.

1127. Walker, Eric A. "The Jameson Raid," Cambridge Historical Journal, vol. 6, no. 3 (1940), 283-306.

1128. _____. "Lord Milner and South Africa," Proceedings of the British Academy, vol. 28 (1942), 155-178.

1129. White, Robert. "Letters from South Africa in 1895," JRAS, vol. 37 (1938), 167-73.

1130. Wilde, Richard H. "Joseph Chamberlain and the South African Republic, 1895-99," AYB, pt. 1 (1956), vii-158.

1131. Williams, Robert. "The Cape to Cairo Railway," JAS, vol. 20 (1920-21), 241-58.

1132. Winkler, Henry R. "Joseph Chamberlain and the Jameson Raid," American Historical Review, vol. 54, no. 4 (July 1949), 841-49.

1133. Woodhouse, C. M. "The Missing Telegrams and the Jameson Raid," <u>History Today</u>, vol. 12 (June 1962), 395-404; vol. 12 (July 1962), 506-14.

<u>See also</u>: II, XX

XXVI   GERMAN IMPERIAL POLICY IN SOUTHERN AFRICA

1134. Aydelotte, William O. "The First German Colony and its Diplomatic Consequences," <u>Cambridge Historical Journal</u>, vol. 5, no. 3 (1937), 291-313.

1135. Hallgarten, Wolfgang. "L'essor et l'échec de la politique boer de l'Allemagne (1890-1898)," <u>Revue Historique</u>, vol. 177, no. 3 (May-June 1936), 505-29.

1136. Penner, C. D. "Germany and the Transvaal before 1896," <u>Journal of Modern History</u>, vol. 12, no. 1 (Mar. 1940), 31-58.

<u>See also</u>: XXII, XXV

AUTHOR INDEX

Boggie, A. - 585
Bokhorst, M. - 705
Bolze, L. W. - 1059
Bond, B. - 969
Boni, N. - 1060
Booth, A. R. - 274
Booyens, B. - 779
Bosch, D. W. - 894
Bosman, D. B. - 706f
Bosman, F.C.L. - 709
Bosman, I. D. - 838
Botha, C. G. - 29, 710-19, 780
Bothma, C. V. - 489
Boucher, M. - 781
Boxer, C. R. - 3, 720
Bradlow, E. - 56, 1097
Bradlow, F. - 56
Breitenbach, J. J. - 782
Breutz, P.-L. - 160, 543-49
Breytenbach, J. H. - 839, 970
Brothwell, D. R. - 100
Brown, R. - 581, 1061
Brownlee, F. - 57, 317, 928
Brownlee, W. T. - 408
Bruwer, J. P. van S. - 1049
Bryant, A. T. - 381, 427
Bryden, H. A. - 4
Bullock, C. - 490
Burn, D. - 143
Burrows, H. R. - 1085
Burton, R. - 681
Burton, T. E. - 681
Butler, J. - 1098
Buxton, E. - 1099
Buys, B. R. - 840
Buys, M. H. - 971

Callaway, Rev. C. H. - 428
Campbell, K. - 30
Campbell, W. B. - 929
Carbutt, C. L. - 582
Carnegie, D. - 583
Carnegie, W. A. - 584
Caton-Thompson, G. - 101, 126, 172-75
Chadwick, J.C.C. - 429
Chidziwa, J. - 619

Franz, G. H. - 469
Fredoux, F. - 552
Frey, C. - 366
Fripp, C. E. - 290, 1107
Fryer, A. K. - 790

Gailey, H. A. Jr. - 791
Gambo, F. - 587
Gann, L. H. - 8
Garbett, G. K. - 628
Garbutt, H. W. - 388
Gardner, G. A. - 130-33
Gardner, T. - 185
Garlake, P. S. - 186f, 1066
Garson, N. G. - 1041
Geyer, A. L. - 731
Geyser, O. - 890, 1108
Gie, S.F.N. - 732
Gilbert, D. W. - 64
Giliomee, H. B. - 792
Glass. S. - 1067
Glover, L. S. - 1068
Gluckman, M. - 389f, 431f
Godée-Molsbergen, E. C. - 733
Godlonton, W. A. - 691f
Goiran, H. - 734
Goodall, E. - 188f
Goodwin, A.J.H. - 109-12, 162, 164, 341ff
Gray, R. - 65f
Greenberg, J. H. - 238-41
Grey, P. C. - 980
Grilo, V.H.V. - 494
Grimsehl, H. W. - 950, 981
Grobbelaar, C. S. - 164
Grobbelaar, J.J.G. - 951
Grönberg, G. - 291
Grylls, R. G. - 898
Guillarmod, A. M. - 470
Guma, S. M. - 471
Guthrie, M. - 242-45

H.M.G.J. - 588
Haasbroek, D.J.P. - 793, 982
Hahn, C.H.L. - 662
Hall, C. G. - 735
Hall, R. N. - 190f, 323

Hallgarten, W. - 1135
Hallowes, D. P. - 248
Hammond, E. - 899
Hammond, J. H. - 1109
Hammond-Tooke, W. D. - 35, 411-17, 433
Hamnett, I. - 472
Hancock, W. K. - 850
Hannan, Rev. - 629
Harlow, V. - 1110
Harrington, A. L. - 851
Hattersley, A. F. - 9, 67, 794f, 852, 891, 900, 1111f
Haupt, D. J. - 983
Heijstek, J.L.K. - 985
Helly, D. O. - 36
Hemans, H. N. - 630
Henochsberg, E. S. - 901
Henry, J. A. - 984
Herrison, C. D. - 796
Hewitt, J. - 344
Heyns, H. A. - 797
Hickman, A. S. - 1069
Hiernaux, J. - 391
Hinde, W. H. - 736
Hirschberg, W. - 324
H.M.G.J. - 588
Hockly, H. E. - 37
Hodgson, M. L. - 345
Hoernlé, A. W. - 346
Hoffmann, A. C. - 139
Hoge, J. - 737-40
Hole, H. M. - 589, 693, 1070
Holleman, J. F. - 434ff
Holli, M. G. - 38
Holm, E. - 113
Holt, B. - 292, 798f, 902, 931f
Honyera, - 631
Hoogenhout, P. G. 325
Hope, C. D. - 68
Hoste, H. F. - 1071
Hove, M. M. - 632
How, M. - 473
Howland, R. C. - 1072
Howman, E. G. - 633
Hughes, A.J.B. - 590
Hugo, M. - 986f
Humphreys, B. - 373
Humphreys, J.C.N. - 39

Hunt, D. R. - 495
Hunt, K. S. - 800
Hunter, M. See Wilson, M.
Hutchinson, B. - 392
Hutton, E. - 903
Huttenback, R. A. - 1089

Immelman, R.F.M. - 741
Inskeep, R. R. - 114
Ireland, A. - 1113

Jackson, F.W.D. - 904
Jacobs, D. S. - 952
Jacques, A. A. - 40
Jaffey, A.J.E. - 192
Jeffreys, M.D.W. - 246, 437, 682
Jenkins, P. L. - 1114
Jod, P. - 367
Jollie, E. T. - 1115
Jones, G. I. - 474
Jones, N. - 193
Jorissen, E.J.P. - 293
Jousse, T. - 475
Junod, H. P. - 393, 438, 677

Kahn, E. - 69f, 988
Kendall, J. - 591f
Keppel-Jones, A. M. - 71
Kies, G.J.A. - 1116
Kingon, J.R.L. - 72f, 394, 419
Kirby, P. R. - 347, 420, 742, 933
Kistner, W. - 989
Koeman, Ir. C. - 743
Köhler, O. - 247, 663-67
Kotzé, D. J. - 439f, 593
Kotze, H. A. - 1019
Kreft, H.H.G. - 368
Kriel, J. D. - 953
Krige, E. J. - 496ff
Krige, J. D. - 496, 499f
Krüger, B. J. - 990ff
Krüger, D. W. - 993
Kruger, F. - 395, 476, 501
Kuit, A. - 994
Kuper, A. J. - 576
Kuper, B. - 41
Kuper, H. - 425, 441f

96

Martineau, J. - 1118
Mason, A. W. - 444
Mason, R. J. - 117, 136ff
Masson, F. - 296
Matthews, Z. K. - 558
Mauch, K. - 639
Mawby, A. A. - 997
Meiring, A.J.D. - 349
Mennell, E. P. - 195
Meredith, L. C. - 640
Meyer, S. - 955
Meyler, H. M. - 445
Mhlanga, W. - 446
Midgely, J. F. - 855
Miracle, M. P. - 397
Moffat, R. L. - 1074
Möller-Malan, D. - 506
Moloja, - 447
Mönnig, H. O. - 11, 507f
Morant, G. M. - 126
Morris, S. E. - 641
Mouton, J. A. - 998
Muhlanga, S. - 642f
Muller, C.F.J. - 43, 746, 805, 856-59
Murray, A. H. - 860
Myburgh, A. C. - 448f

Naidoo, V. S. - 1090
Naudé, C.P.T. - 44, 77
Naude, S. D. - 747
Ncube, R.M.M. - 596
Neal, W. G. - 190
Nell, P. R. - 999
Nettleton, G. E. - 559
Newitt, M.D.D. - 694
Nhlapo, J. M. - 450
Nienaber, G. S. - 259, 350ff
Nienaber, P. J. - 12f
Nobbs, E. A. - 644, 806
Norton, Rev. - 482
Norton, G. R. - 398
Norton, W. A. - 260, 399, 483, 1051
Nyembezi, C.L.S. - 451

Oberholster, J. J. - 372f
Oberholster, M. O. - 452

Okoye, F.N.C. - 453
Oliver, H. G. - 807
Oliver, R. - 400
O'Mahoney, K. E. - 1075
O'Neil, Rev. - 597
Otto, J. C. - 509ff, 1000
Oudard, G. - 1119

P. C. G. - 937
Pachai, B. - 1091
Park, M. - 910
Partridge, T. C. - 139
Pauw, B. A. - 560
Paver, F. R. - 140
Pelzer, A. N. - 14f, 1001ff
Penner, C. D. - 1136
Perrot, C-H. - 484f
Pettman, C. - 78ff, 353f
Pieterse, D. J. - 1004, 1120f
Pigott, W. H. - 808
Pitout, J. A. - 598f
Ploeger, J. - 297, 748, 861ff, 911f, 956, 1005-11
Pollett, H. - 1076
Poole, E.H.L. - 454
Posselt, F.W.T. - 600f, 645ff
Potgieter, E. F. - 81, 512
Potgieter, F. J. - 1012
Preller, G. - 842
Pretorius, H. S. - 1013
Pretorius, J. G. - 864
Price, T. - 695
Prinsloo, C. W. - 505
Pullen, R. A. - 148
Punt, W. - 865f

Rademeyer, J. I. - 513, 602
Ranger, T. - 1077, 1122
Ransford, D. N. - 1078
Raum, O. F. - 422, 749
Raven-Hart, R. - 298-301, 355, 684, 750f
Rea, W. F. - 696, 1079
Read, M. - 455f
Rennie, J.V.L. - 809
Reuter, F. - 514
Reyburn, H. A. - 810
Reyneke, C.J.J. - 1014f

Reyneke, G. J. - 1016
Rita-Ferreira, A. - 678
Robb, A. M. - 82
Roberts, M. - 811
Roberts, N. - 515
Robertson, H. M. - 83f, 752-56, 913
Robins, P. A. - 196
Robinson, A. M. L. - 302, 356, 812ff
Robinson, K. R. - 177, 180, 197-206, 220, 648
Rochlin, S. A. - 303f, 374ff, 685, 815, 893, 1017
Roodt-Coetzee, K. - 867
Roos, J. de V. - 757f
Rose, J. H. - 816
Rosenthal, E. - 85
Routh, C.R.N. - 868
Rudner, I. - 141, 165
Rudner, J. - 165f
Rust, F. - 1052
Rust, H. J. - 561
Rutherford, G. - 759
Ruzicka, K. F. - 305

Salomon, L. - 86
Sandler, E. M. - 957
Saunders, C. C. - 562
Savage, M. B. - 914
Sayce, R. U. - 87
Schapera, I. - 45, 262, 333, 357, 401, 563-75, 669, 686, 1018
Schauder, H. - 88
Schmidt, P. W. - 334
Schofield, J. F. - 46, 118, 156ff, 162, 167, 185, 207-11, 697
Scholtz, G. D. - 16
Scholtz, P. L. - 760
Schoute-Vanneck, C. A. - 159
Schrire, C. - 168
Schutte, C.E.G. - 377
Secretariat of U.N. - 378
Seddon, J. D. - 142
Seed, J. H. - 649f
Sentker, H. F. - 119
Seruya, S. - 698
Seymour, J. - 670
Seymour, L. F. - 651
Siegrist, M. K. - 143
Silberbauer, G. B. - 576
Silva Rego, A. da. - 699f

Simons, H. J. - 402f
Simpson, D. H. - 47
Smit, D. E. - 89
Smit, J. J. - 457
Smith, A. H. - 761
Smith, D.J.G. - 1019
Smith, E. W. - 486
Smith, H. S. - 652
Smith, K. W. - 516
Soga, J. H. - 423
Spies, F. J. du T. - 17, 306, 869
Spilhaus, M. W. - 762
Spohr, O. H. - 48, 817
Stals, E. L. P. - 1053
Stander, H. - 458
Stapelton, F. - 211
Stayt, H. A. - 517
Stead, W. H. - 653
Steyn, J. L. - 49
Steytler, F. A. - 818
Stigand, A. G. - 577
Stock, J.L.W. - 763
Stokes, E. - 1123f
Strydom, S. - 18
Stuart, P. A. - 459
Stuiver, M. - 120
Summers, R. - 121, 180, 195, 212-20, 590, 603, 618
Swanepoel, H. L. - 764
Swart, M. J. - 90

Taberer, W. S. - 654
Tabler, E. C. - 50, 307-15, 1080f
Tagwireyi, J. H. - 655
Tapson, R. R. - 656
Taylor, A. R. - 51
Taylor, G. A. - 604
Taylor, H. J. - 605
Terry, E. - 671
Thom, H. B. - 870f
Thompson, J. B. - 645
Thompson, L. C. - 122, 518
Thompson, L. M. - 19f, 91, 958, 1092
Tizirai, P. - 657
Tobias, P. V. - 335ff, 358
Tomlinson, F. R. - 1019
'Transvaal Lawyer' - 1020
Trapido, S. - 819, 915, 938

Wagner, G. - 673
Walker, E. - 94ff, 1082, 1127f
Wallenberg, J. - 316
Wallis, J.P.R. - 608
Walls, A. F. - 53
Walton, J. - 150-55, 161, 222f
Warhurst, P. R. - 680, 1083
Weidemann, N. C. - 1036
Wellington, J. H. - 97
Wells, L. H. - 185
Werner, A. - 266
Wessels, J. W. - 98
Westphal, E.O.J. - 267ff
Wheeler-Holohan, V. - 925
Wheelwright, C. A. - 465
White, F. - 224
Whate, R. - 1129
Whitton, F. E. - 926
Whitty, A. - 196, 220, 225-28
Wichmann, F.A.F. - 887f
Wiid, J. A. - 99
Wilde, R. H. - 1130
Wilhelm, J. H. - 674
Willcox, A. R. - 363
Williams, R. - 1131
Wilson, M. - 10, 418, 424
Wilson, N. W. - 832
Winkler, H. - 1132
Winter, J. A. - 539ff
Wood, W. S. - 889
Woodhouse, C. M. - 1133
Woods, G.G.B. - 609f
Wright, E. B. - 407
Wypkema, A. - 1037

Young, L. M. - 927